Advance Praise for "Nowhere Near First"

"Cory Reese writes with humor, humbleness and honesty. His story is both uplifting and real, and his tales of persistence and perseverance are sure to inspire, whether you're at the front of the pack or nowhere near first. Regardless of the title, this book's a winner!"

~ Dean Karnazes, author of Ultramarathon Man: Confessions of an All-Night Runner

"Cory mixes in his unmistakable humor and detail into a few dozen short chapters that can be read all at once or spread out over time. From his tear-jerking teenage years with his father to running races dressed as Mexican wrestlers to the fine art of balancing ultra-training and family life, Cory paints a real-life picture of a normal, passionate guy in a crazy sport filled with other fun characters. If you're just starting out on your running path, you'll have a better understanding of what you're getting into, and if you're a grizzled ultra veteran, you'll connect to the details and emotions of this wacky sport."

~ Eric Schranz, Host, Ultrarunnerpodcast

"Cory Reese's book, Nowhere Near First, is an immensely entertaining and profoundly educational story about overcoming challenges to forge a meaningful life. As it recounts his ultrarunning exploits in funny and insightful ways, his story and experiences are universal and relevant to all readers as they pursue their dreams and face the inevitable suffering and setbacks along the way. Reese's story is must-read for people looking to find meaning and purpose in modern-day society, and as they choose the paths and actions that will define the 21st Century. Read this book. You will enjoy it, and it will make the world a better place for everyone."

~ Karl Hoagland, Publisher, UltraRunning Magazine

"Nowhere Near First is a book about an ordinary guy doing extraordinary things. The point isn't just Cory. The point is you can actually do this yourself."

~ Vanessa Runs, author of The Summit Seeker and Daughters of Distance

"Cory has penned a very personal account of overcoming hardship in his personal and athletic life. Nowhere Near First tells his story of perseverance and survival in a vivid, down and dirty way that peaks with his extraordinarily positive way of looking at life."

~ Marshall Ulrich, author of Running On Empty: An Ultramarathoner's Story of Love, Loss, and a Record-Setting Run Across America

"Running 100 miles is like living for a year: You're up, you're down, you experience the full spectrum of life's greatest joys and challenges. 'Fast Cory' may not finish at the front of the pack, but he knows how to make the most of running--and of life--as well as just about anyone I know. A refreshingly honest mix of narrative and lessons learned, Nowhere Near First is a compelling read that teaches runners and non-runners about our beloved sport--and, more importantly, about becoming more resilient, being present for our family and friends, and living life to its fullest."

~ Travis Macy, ultra runner, endurance coach, and author of The Ultra Mindset: An Endurance Champion's 8 Core Principles for Success in Business, Sports, and Life

Nowhere Near First

Ultramarathon Adventures
From The Back Of The Pack

By Cory Reese

Edited by Jill Homer
Cover photograph by Jeremiah Barber
Moon photograph by Alex Chamberlain
All other photographs by Cory Reese
Cover design by Marius Design
Interior design by Penoaks Publishing, http://penoaks.com

Table of Contents

Foreword

There once was a runner named Cory
with him, running never was a borey.
He ran kind of slow so he called himself fast;
he made a name for himself by having a blast.

It is human nature to seek the exceptional. Runners are not exempt from this desire. We put the accomplished athletes—Killian Jornet, Scott Jurek, Dean Karnazes, Emilie Forsberg, Shalene Flanagan, Meb Keflezighi—high on pedestals, where we can admire their speed, their dedication, and their sheer physical talent. In performance, they are the best of us.

Yet we, *we* being the majority of the running population, will not excel in running enough to have a career from it. Let's face it, some of us, well…. are actually kind of terrible at it. Despite the blaring fact that we aren't going to be getting anything more than a finisher's medal *(and sometimes not even that!)* we wake up early in the morning, before our kids are awake, or our college roommate has finished shaking off their hangover, to run. Or we run and skip a party, or we run instead of eating lunch, or we run late at night while we watch the moon rise….We rub our eyes, we go outside. We run and we see.

We don't know how to not be a runner.

In truth, we're all different types of runners.

It was clear that I had no innate running talent when I first started running. I was in the back of the pack of every 5k race I entered in junior high and high school. I loved it there. There were no expectations of me besides running as I pleased. I got to miss school and ride a bus with my friends to a meet. We'd stretch and talk and warm-up and meet new people. There is an instant kinship between runners, even if they are competitors, even at a young age.

Then, we ran. I had a hard time focusing on racing. As I darted across the grass, I was distracted by the way the sunrays stretched and reached between the leaves. After 2 miles, I caught up to a friend who had resigned to walking. I belted out a Disney song, and started telling my best blonde jokes. I wasn't going to be scoring any points for the team, so I decided to walk it in with her. I loved running for all that it encompassed…the people, the places, the motion, the emotion. Frankly, I didn't know how to not run. I also didn't know *how to run*, which is potentially why I lacked the foot-speed to be a competitor. I discovered that being a runner, and knowing how to run, were two different things. Innately I was one, but it took years of hard work to learn the latter.

I met Cory much later in life. It was Thanksgiving, and I was near St. George, Utah for a holiday rock climbing trip. Since we were social media pals *(isn't this the modern equivalent of BFFs?)* I let him know I was in the area and wanted to familiarize myself with local trails and runners, and he obliged by arranging a run. Our small group consisted of four different runners—each with different paces, skill sets, and trail preferences—which quickly melded into a group of friends sharing dreams, ideas, and stories. Cory wanted to run a 100 miler every month for a year the following year. Another runner wanted to run fast, to push his potential racing the "shorter" ultra distances. The other member of our group wanted to grow the community of running as part of a local race directing team. I meagerly added my dreams of playing on mountaintops, as I was still trying to figure out where I fit into the sport with my passion for long mountain link-ups and lesser-known routes. These niche difference in our passion for running—they united us. First place and "DFL" (Dead F*ing Last, aka Deserving Full Lionization) were represented on our run. I was reminded how we, as runners, are united by the common thread of the ground we run on… Or perhaps that thread is passion that drives us to run.

In this memoir, Cory speaks with humor and wit by not taking himself too seriously, while maintaining the intense passion for the sport that has become an adjective to so many of us. Cory is a magnet in the running community—perhaps because he lives authentically as his own lovable, quirky self. He runs because he loves to—so, he runs what he wants to. He's been known to come up with witty, terrible ideas, like running 100 miles fueled on Hostess products, suffering through 100 miles on a track alone in the scorching heat of a desert summer, or running to all of the local ice cream shops for 40 miles of paved hell… and he shares the dark, funny, and powerful moments. His "bad ideas" are also incredible feats of human ability, and though they lack the pedestal speed of the elites…His stories are far more entertaining to read about, and more grounding to reflect upon.

It is in the uniqueness of a singular that we find the connections and correlations to pieces of our own lives. Not all runners run the distances that Cory talks about. Not all runners run as quickly, or as slowly, as he or I or each other. But we can share the meaning we find in the moments spent running, we can make each other laugh, we can grow. If runners are judged by the quality of their character (or entertainment value of their character, for that matter…) rather than the paces or distances they run, Cory would be judged as the best of us.

This book reminds us of what it is to be a runner. It's not about running fast; it's not about running slow. Occasionally running is for competition, other times running is for therapy, more frequently running is for play… but most often, it's innate. We cannot help it, even if we are "terrible" at it. We run not because we want to, but because we have to. We are runners, and so, we run. We know of no other way to live. The tall tales, the laughter, the vast life that is contained in the camaraderie of the world that is *running*, filled with the beautiful people we call *runners*, this is what Cory has captured with his words.

~ Jennilyn Eaton, www.themountainist.com

1) Introduction

At least my eyelashes didn't hurt

D o you want a quesadilla?"
Somewhere within the deep recesses of my brain, I understood that someone was asking me a question. The most primitive part of my brain also understood that generally the most polite thing to do when someone asks you a question is to provide an answer. But formulating an answer to such a complex question was beyond my current capabilities.

It was dark outside and frigid air was stinging my cheeks. I stood in place, looking straight ahead in a daze. The left side of her mouth rose with a grin, and again the volunteer at the aid station looked me in the eyes and repeated her question.

"Do you want a quesadilla?"

I don't remember my response. All I knew was that moments later I found myself walking down the trail with a quesadilla in my hand. I didn't have the slightest sense of hunger but nibbled on the warm triangle of food because that's what you're supposed to do when someone puts food in your hand.

I was in the middle of the Across The Years seventy-two-hour race in Phoenix, Arizona. Aside from a few short catnaps, my body had been in forward motion for more than sixty hours. My sleep-deprived mind was numb and struggling to process information. At a race like Across The Years, a weary mind is nothing more than a minimal inconvenience. Cognitively, runners must only understand one very simple concept: keep … moving … forward.

Years of running had prepared me for this race. In the previous five years, I had run a few 5K races. As many runners can attest, a 5K is merely a planted seed which later blooms into a desire to run a half marathon, and then a marathon. I ran a steady diet of half marathons, and then marathons, and then fifty-milers, and then hundred-milers. But Across The Years was a different beast; an intimidating, unknown, terrifying beast.

Almost all races have one thing in common: a finish line. Runners begin at a starting line, and each step they take brings them closer to the finish line. The body and mind have a comprehension of how far they have traveled, and how much farther they have to go before they can stop.

Across The Years is different. Instead of a fixed distance race, it is a timed race. Runners circle a one-mile loop as many times as they can within a fixed amount of time. I chose the seventy-two-hour race. At the same time I was running, there were other runners competing in a twenty-four-hour race, a forty-eight-hour race, and an unfathomable six-day race.

For three days, that one-mile loop was my only focus. Loop. Loop. Eat. Loop. Loop. Loop. Drink. "Wait. Did I take a salt tablet on the last lap ... or was that five hours ago?" Loop. Loop. "Wow. That runner looks like he's part of the zombie apocalypse." Loop. Loop. Loop. "I look like I'm part of the zombie apocalypse!"

While my mind had become numb many, many hours before, my body certainly hadn't. My feet were puffy. When I took my shoes off to change my socks, it looked as though someone had secretly replaced my toes with Vienna Sausages. The bottoms of my feet felt as though I was walking across molten lava.

Early in the race, I would stop to remove pebbles from my shoes, only to realize that I didn't have pebbles in my shoes. What felt like rocks were actually the beginnings of blisters. Those pebbles later felt like stones, which later felt like rough, sharp boulders.

My knees were stiff and sore. I looked less like a runner and more like the Tin Man creaking down the Yellow Brick Road toward Oz. Though the aid station had nearly everything a runner could want, it was sorely lacking in an oil can for rusty knees. Hips. Back. Neck. Ouch. Loop. Loop. Loop. My eyes stung from a layer of dust that had collected on my contact lenses over the previous days. It felt as though my eyelashes were the only part of my body that wasn't hurting. Loop. Loop. But none of those things — NONE of those things — mattered. Beyond the pain, soreness, and fatigue, one purpose remained: keep ... moving ... forward.

There was a goal in my relentless forward progress. Not only did I want to run a seventy-two-hour race to push my body to the limit and see how much it was capable of, but in my heart of hearts I wanted to see if I could complete two-hundred miles in that amount of time. While the goal seemed possible at the onset, I knew that my race would need to go nearly flawlessly for this to happen. Unfortunately the race hadn't gone flawlessly. I had an unmistakable diagnosis of Boulders-In-Shoes-Walking-On-Lava-With-Tin-Man-Knees Syndrome. Still, I wasn't going down without a fight.

Loop.

Loop.

Loop.

Keep.

Moving.

Forward.

In an ultramarathon, at some point along the way you cross a line where pain becomes your companion. Suffering becomes part of the journey. Sometimes the suffering is minor, and other times it is nearly unbearable … but it always comes. Fortunately, I had one ace up my sleeve. I knew how to suffer.

2) The Electric Wheelchair Through Target

Across The Years, 2015

Before Across The Years, I had never run farther than one-hundred miles. I knew I wanted to shoot for finishing two-hundred miles during the three-day race, but I had no idea what to expect physically and mentally beyond the hundred-mile distance. Would my brain explode inside my skull? Would my legs be worn down to nothing more than stumps, leaving a bloody trail behind me by the end of the race? From previous ultramarathons, I knew that after running one-hundred miles, my body often felt like I had been standing on a train full of dynamite that had accidentally exploded. It was nearly impossible to fathom how it would be humanly possible to continue moving for another hundred miles after that point.

To prepare, I consulted with some of the top ultrarunners in the country who have experience running hundreds of miles at a time: Mark Hellenthal and Mike Miller, who had both run two-hundred-plus miles in seventy-two hours; Yolanda Holder, who completed four-hundred miles at a six-day race in Alaska earlier in the year; Ed Ettinghausen, who ran 476 miles in the six-day race at Across The Years one year earlier; and Joe Fejes, who won the six-day race the previous year by running a remarkable 555 miles.

These runners gave me some great tips on race strategy (be willing to embrace pain, and keep moving forward no matter what the pace); nutrition (don't pass up the macaroni and cheese they serve at the aid station because it is basically amazing); and sleep (plan on four hours or less per night, only lay down when you are sleep walking, and get back up if you don't fall asleep within ten minutes). It was incredibly helpful to tap into a wealth of experience from people who weren't deterred by goals that some would consider impossible.

Across The Years is held on a one-mile loop around the spring training facilities for the White Sox and Dodgers. The surface of the course is dirt and crushed rock, with a short dose of pavement, and almost no elevation gain. The first time I circled the loop, I saw a beautiful pond that we would be passing with each mile. Not knowing what to expect in the coming days, I was scared that after sleep deprivation set in, I would imagine a killer whale in there, and then I would jump in to Free Willy. After days of uninterrupted running, anything seemed possible.

My friends "Shacky" Shackleford and Vanessa Runs live in their RV and roam the country in search of beautiful scenery and awesome trails. They came to Across The Years and parked their RV next to the course. I laughed every time I passed by it. In bold, blue letters scrawled across the back of the RV, a message read "Never trust a fart in an ultra."

Aside from the advice "Don't pass up the macaroni and cheese," I wasn't sure how to handle nutrition for a race beyond a hundred miles. I decided I'd approach nutrition the same way I had in previous races, by getting most of my fuel from liquid calories. I've become convinced that liquid calories are the way to go when running ultra distances. I used primarily Tailwind Nutrition, a powder with calories and electrolytes, mixed with water. You have to be careful how you transport Tailwind, however. I put the sweet, white powder in little baggies that I can quickly add to bottles of water. If I was pulled over by the police, I would undoubtedly be suspected as a cocaine dealer with all of my little baggies of white powder.

I supplemented the Tailwind with other liquid calories such as Coke and nectar directly from heaven (also known as Dr. Pepper). When I felt hungry, I would eat small amounts of food from the aid station so I didn't overload my stomach. There is nothing worse than battling a stomachache during a race. Over the course of the three days, I ate lasagna, pizza, lots of Ramen noodles, and enough M&Ms to feed the entire country of Singapore.

I brought my secret weapon to the race: my son Jackson. He was thirteen years old and had caught the ultrarunning bug. He loved joining my wife to crew at races, loved volunteering at aid stations, and loved the infectious atmosphere of the events. He was ecstatic when I asked if he wanted to come to Arizona with me. At the race, he joined me on laps every once in a while, helped prepare bottles of Tailwind to drink, and got supplies and clothes as needed. He also helped keep me moving forward by providing updates to football bowl games, or mocking me for how slow I was walking.

My plan for the first night was to not sleep at all. After doing a number of hundred-mile races, I had learned what I need to do to get through a night without sleep, so I figured I'd get through it okay. I got a bit sleepy at times, but eventually got through the night to see the first sunrise of the race.

After twenty-four hours, I had completed ninety miles. When I reached one-hundred miles on day two, I broke down and cried. It wasn't the kind of crying where a few tears leak out of your eyes. It was the kind of crying that takes your breath away as your nose starts producing snot bubbles. I was feeling tired and worn out, both physically and mentally. I cried because I couldn't fathom how it would be possible to go another hundred miles. It simply did not seem possible. I'm not a very emotional person, but at this point in time, my emotions were raw.

I gave myself a pep talk. I reminded myself that I didn't need to go one-hundred more miles. I only needed to put one step in front of the other. Looking into the future or doing math about your pace can be incredibly demoralizing and discouraging during an ultramarathon. It's critical to stay focused on just running the mile you're in. After a few miles, I had pulled out of my funk and felt better.

I have some debilitating nerve issues in my feet during every hundred-miler. It's an enormously painful neuropathy that makes each step hurt. I've felt it during every single hundred-miler I've ever run. The pain usually starts around mile sixty, and feels like I'm walking on red hot coals. Every single step feels like pressing my feet against needles. This pain kicked in with a fury during Across The Years. In my mind, I assumed that this foot pain was just part of the experience for everyone. I thought this was normal. I figured "You're running a hundred miles. Of course your feet are going to hurt, dummy!"

During Across The Years, I had the opportunity to spend some miles with very experienced ultrarunners. I asked if they experienced something similar, and what they do about it. Every single response was something like, "Wow, that sounds terrible! I can't imagine running with pain like that. Of course my feet get sore, but nothing like that."

I was surprised to learn that this wasn't normal. (Since that time, I have visited with a number of different doctors to try and target the problem. I have tried various medications, creams, lubricants, shoes, socks, and inserts. The problem continues, but I haven't given up trying to find a solution.) Running on burning hot coals for ten hours of a hundred-miler is one thing. Running on burning hot coals for fifty hours at Across The Years dramatically increased the difficulty level of the race.

By 11 p.m. on the second day, I was fully entrenched in sleep walking, considering that I hadn't slept at all since the race started thirty-eight hours earlier. I decided I would lay in my tent with an alarm set to wake me up in two hours. I took off my shoes, got in my sleeping bag, and rested my head on my pillow. Then I noticed that, for some reason, Jackson was squeezing my feet.

With a stern voice of frustration I said loudly, "Jackson, stop squeezing my feet!" But he didn't listen. He kept squeezing them. I sat up to yell at him … and then noticed that the tent was empty. I was feeling my heartbeat in my feet! With every pump of my heart, it felt like someone was squeezing my feet. It was the most bizarre sensation I have ever experienced.

I was astounded that I didn't need the whole two hours to sleep. After an hour and thirty-five minutes, my eyes popped open and I felt completely refreshed! It didn't seem possible. In everyday life, I don't function well if I'm short on sleep, but during the race I seemed to be doing fine with minimal sleep.

Coaxing my body back into forward motion after sleeping for a while was a challenge. My legs felt like they had gone through a metamorphosis during my sleep. But instead of a caterpillar turning into a butterfly, my legs had turned into cinder blocks. Another runner caught up with me and asked how I was doing.

"Well, I just woke up from my first nap of the race. I've never slept in the middle of a race before so I don't know what to expect, but right now my legs are really, really stiff," I said.

She laughed and said, "Don't worry, that's normal. Give it two miles and you'll be completely loosened up again."

I was skeptical, but within a few miles I was pleasantly surprised to find that she was right.

The cold temperatures during the night were intense. Chilly winter air pierced through every layer of clothing I was wearing and froze my body to the core. It can be difficult to regulate electrolytes during ultramarathons. Consequently, temperatures are magnified. When it's hot outside, the heat is felt more intensely. When it's cold outside, the frigid temperatures are felt more intensely. I brought more layers than I thought I would need, and ended up using all of them.

I started sleep-walking again early in the morning. If I didn't know better, I'd swear I had been injected with an elephant tranquilizer. I treated the whole sleeping issue like a science project.

"I wonder how I would feel if I set my alarm to wake up in thirty minutes." So I gave it a try. I woke up after only sixteen minutes, again feeling fully refreshed. It was like my body just needed enough time to flip off the light switch and then flip it back on. It was fascinating to see what my body was capable of accomplishing.

After forty-eight hours, I had completed 155 miles. It was then that I finally started to believe that two-hundred miles was possible. Jackson came out with me for some laps on the third morning. He was such a great support and seemed to genuinely be having fun. (He ended up doing a total of twenty miles with me during the race.) To keep warm, I wore a sock monkey hat that my daughter Kylee had given me years before. Having that small sense of family connection helped me when times got tough.

It is difficult to describe how demanding the third day and night were. Every muscle in my legs was twisted up in knots that I just couldn't unkink. I tried rubbing my legs, stretching, and using a foam roller. Nothing helped. In all the ultramarathons I had run, I never experienced anything like the way I was feeling.

The third night was ridiculously colder than the ridiculously cold second night. I brought the same clothes that have gotten me through winter hundred-milers. I brought heavy jackets. I even brought my heaviest winter coat just in case. I had all of those layers on, and I was still feeling like a freezer-burned popsicle.

I wore Altra Paradigm shoes for the first hundred miles, then Altra One2 shoes after that. I also used Injinji socks, which had worked well to prevent blisters at many previous races. I read good reviews about a different brand of socks, so I figured I'd try them on the third night. Try something new when you're attempting to run two-hundred miles for the first time? Very foolish. That was the dumbest thing I'd done in a long time. (Closely followed by the time I inhaled two large chili dogs the night before a hundred-miler a few years earlier.) After only two miles, the socks were causing problems and it felt like someone jabbed an ice pick into the top of my foot. This led to a thirty-minute hobble to the medical tent, where I saw that I had given birth to a sixth toe. The blister was big enough to need a birth certificate. I changed back to my regular socks, which were becoming uncomfortably snug around the toes because of swelling. Unfortunately, by then the damage was done. I couldn't undo the "Oh crap. I have a sixth toe" problem.

I felt a bit disappointed that I didn't see any Care Bears during my run. The closest I came to hallucinating was during the third night. I decided that in an effort to stay awake, I would listen to an ESPN podcast. I heard the hosts talking, but my brain was greatly struggling to comprehend the conversation they were having. I knew the words they were saying, but I just didn't understand the meaning of all the words strung together. Even though I recognized that this was just a regular conversation they were having, it felt like the radio hosts were talking so incomprehensibly fast that my brain just couldn't keep up. I ended up turning it off since I couldn't understand what they were saying.

After sixty-eight hours and thirty-four minutes, something happened that I would have never imagined in my wildest dreams when I first started running years ago — I finished two-hundred miles. Even now, I get goosebumps thinking about that moment when I reached two hundred. Jackson had done the lap with me, and congratulated me when I reached two hundred. I was so thankful to have my son there with me.

Runners cross a timing mat after each loop, and a big screen shows their mileage. The timing mat is at the headquarters where volunteers sit during the entire race to monitor the timing system. The sight at the timing station after finishing two-hundred miles was magical. Guess who was there to see our finish? Nobody! No spectators, no runners, no crew … nobody. Even the timing guys were fast asleep. I truly love this about ultramarathons. Usually, there are no cheering crowds. No external rewards. Just that internal satisfaction of knowing you persevered amidst challenges, and didn't give up.

Jackson and I stood there alone in the dark, and I gave him a big hug. I felt my eyes start to leak as I said, "Thank you Jackson. Thank you for being here with me."

I was so tired that I kept falling asleep mid-stride. Then I would stumble myself awake fifty yards down the trail and not know how I got there. I needed to rest. I decided I'd sleep for an hour and then get in a few more miles. Before lying down, I went into the heating tent to warm up. I was frozen to the core. A large, covered canopy sat next to the aid station and medical tent. Hard, metal chairs were placed throughout the room and large propane heaters blew air that felt like warm rays of sunshine.

Let me tell you about this heating tent. This is where you see intense, penetrating exhaustion. It is at least as much of a suffering tent as it is a heating tent. What I continually found remarkable was seeing people sitting in the tent beyond exhaustion — frozen, weary, broken. And then, somehow, they gathered the determination and perseverance to get back out on the trail. My fellow runners were an enormous inspiration.

After a few minutes in the tent, I went to my car and slept for a bit while the heater blew warm air. It was extremely difficult getting my body moving again after the break. I went back on the course and kept pushing with the minimal time I had remaining in the race. When I finished 204 miles, I said, "Okay, I'm done."

Vanessa, the proud owner of the "Never trust a fart in an ultra" RV, came up and said, "There are a few more minutes left in the race. Let's go do one more loop. I'll come out with you." I couldn't pass up her offer. We hurried to finish the last lap before the race ended, and I finished the seventy-two hours with a total of 205 miles. I was barely able to work up enough courage to try a finish line jumping picture.

A tragic thing happened a few hours later. I needed some Band-Aids and Neosporin to doctor up the large blister I had given birth to. Jackson and I went to Target, but my legs were functioning at zero percent. I sat in the parking lot as waves of dread washed over me. I told Jackson, "I don't think there is any way I'll be able to make it from the parking lot to the store. And there is no way I'll be able to walk across the store to get to the stuff I need."

It was a funny thought to realize that I could run 205 miles, but walking from the parking lot to the store was an insurmountable distance. Jackson said, "Dad, I know! You can just ride one of those electric wheelchairs!"

Riding an electric wheelchair was not a life choice I wanted to make, but I saw no other option. I held tightly onto Jackson as I hobbled into the store, and couldn't imagine what people must have been thinking when they saw me leaning on my son. Inside the store, I straddled one of the motorized scooters. On an "Embarrassing Scale" of one to ten, I'd rate this moment a forty-two. (Although it was a pretty smooth ride!)

Jackson howled with laughter and said, "I've got to get a picture of this to send to mom." I decided to add the picture to the race report on my blog as well. (On a related note, a few months later I was casually flipping through the pages of the latest issue of UltraRunning Magazine. A few pages into the issue, I turned a page and saw this very picture of me riding a motorized scooter through Target thanks to former editor John Medinger. It was a complete surprise. Now I was the one howling with laughter.)

* * *

My legs and feet were terribly sore for a few days after the race. It looked like I had replaced every one of my toes with fat sausage links. And my appetite was remarkably ravenous. I ate so many cupcakes and cookies that I was convinced my bloodstream had become sixty-percent frosting. For weeks, I couldn't stop thinking about what an amazing experience this was. I'd wake up in the night, and for a split second I'd think, "Okay, I need to put my shoes back on and get out of the tent to start running again."

During that 205-mile journey, I had this light bulb moment where I realized that we can't know how much we're capable of unless we really push our limits and challenge the beliefs we have about ourselves. Here is the reality: We are capable of so much more than we know. An ultramarathon is an opportunity to share the trail with people who are willing to push past the limits and do something amazing. An ultramarathon strips down your defenses and lets you see a part of yourself that you've never known before. I will never be the same.

3) I Learned How To Suffer

The formative years

I don't remember what Lee Mitchell's face looked like. But I haven't forgotten his legs. Upon writing the previous sentence, I recognize that this is a rather strange thing to say about my Scoutmaster.

I had just turned twelve years old and joined the Boy Scouts program in my Sandy, Utah, neighborhood. I showed up at Lee's house for an activity with my other friends in Scouts. Lee wore bright, white shoes with a Velcro strap across the top. His black shorts came down to his knees, showing tan, muscular calves.

Tucked into Lee's black shorts was a T-shirt with faded white letters that read "Deseret News Marathon." I understood what "Deseret News" meant. That was the local newspaper. But I didn't understand what the word "Marathon" meant. I asked one of my friends.

"Oh, it's a race. Lee runs marathons. It's like twenty-six miles."

At that age, twenty-six miles was a completely arbitrary number. The extent of my running knowledge was that we sometimes ran a hundred-yard dash at school. I had no idea how far a mile was, let alone twenty-six of them.

While my father and my friends' fathers were being betrayed by middle age, with accompanying pants that fit tighter than they used to, Lee was athletic and fit. And those calves looked like steel beams.

The energetic athleticism of Lee Mitchell was a stark contrast to the health struggles that were being experienced at my house.

* * *

One night after returning home from a seventh-grade activity, I walked in the front door of my house and saw my mom and sister standing at the top of the stairs with a concerned look. I immediately felt a sinking feeling in my stomach.

"What's wrong?" I asked.

My mom said, "Your dad is having an insulin reaction. He isn't doing very good. The ambulance is coming."

"What? An ambulance?" I had always known that my dad was diabetic, but the extent of my knowledge about the disease was that there were vials of insulin in the refrigerator and a bag of insulin syringes underneath the bathroom sink. I couldn't understand what could possibly be going on that would require assistance from an ambulance.

"You should go talk to him," she said.

I walked into my parent's bedroom to see my dad tucked neatly into the bed. When he saw me, a smile spread across his face and he raised two fingers in the air. With an upbeat tone he said, "Peace baby!"

I waved back. "Hi dad, I just got home. Are you okay?" Despite his good mood, I could tell that he was confused and disoriented. Minutes later, the red lights of an ambulance were flashing in the driveway and my dad was taken into the cold winter night on a stretcher.

I didn't realize it at the time, but my parents' relationship was frayed and about to tear. That frayed relationship would later end with divorce. My brother, sister, and I all stayed in the same house with my dad. There were the practical reasons for staying there with him: not having to change schools, not having to find new friends, not having to uproot. But more than that, my dad was my best friend. I trusted, respected, and admired him. He had a sense of humor that made him a hit with my friends. He was friendly, giving, and kind.

In my mind, one particular experience solidified how fortunate I was to have him for my dad. We had gone to a cake auction to raise money for a local Cub Scout troop. Everyone in the troop brought a cake to be auctioned. The cakes ranged from elaborately decorated masterpieces to mangled messes of crumbs and frosting. My siblings and I were elated when dad bid the highest amount thus far to buy a cake decorated like the Utah Jazz basketball player John Stockton. The cake was large and the detail of the design was intricate. I was proud of my dad for what I suspected was an act of giving to financially help the Scout troop. For good measure, he bought another cake after that.

Later my pride swelled to an astronomical level. Toward the end of the evening my friend Butch's cake was put up for auction. Butch's family was in ruins. They struggled financially and were barely hovering above poverty. Neither of Butch's parents came to the cake auction. His cake was small and disheveled. The design consisted of some icing with a small donut on top. I remember feeling embarrassed for Butch. If you had been looking at all the cakes at the auction and playing the game "Which Of These Things Is Not Like The Others," it would have been Butch's cake.

The bidding began on Butch's cake. Silence penetrated the air and each second seemed to take an eternity. Then, from the corner of my eye, I saw my dad's hand raise. He bid an amount that was higher than the John Stockton masterpiece. The auctioneer yelled "Sold!" and Butch's face beamed with a smile that couldn't be contained after his cake became the highest selling cake of the entire night. That night, my brother, sister, and I each went home with a cake from the auction. We also left with the complete conviction that our father was the greatest man alive.

* * *

It wasn't long after my mother moved out that my father's health declined rapidly. It was as though his health was a dam cracking with pressure, which burst once the divorce was final. There was another trip to the hospital after I found him unresponsive in a diabetic coma. As his health continued to spiral downward, he developed an ulcer on his foot. Despite aggressive interventions from his doctors, over the course of weeks and months the ulcer continued to grow and became a gaping hole in his foot.

He didn't tell his children much about what his treatment for this entailed. But I overheard him talking with his sisters about how difficult this was physically and emotionally. There were tears in his eyes as he talked about visits where doctors would scrape away the dead, gangrene skin, leaving his flesh raw and bloody. By this time he couldn't wear a shoe anymore. His foot was wrapped in an Ace bandage and he had to use crutches when he walked.

My bedroom was across the hallway from his. One night when he thought the kids were asleep, I heard him in his room crying. His pain was agonizing, engulfing and smothering. As I sat on my bed listening to his suffering across the hall, I closed my eyelids tight. I prayed to wake up and find that this horrible moment was only a dream. I closed my eyelids tighter, and tighter still. But the crying across the hall didn't stop, and soon, despite my clamped eyelids, tears began to flow from my eyes as well.

My thirteen-year old-mind couldn't grasp what was happening. What he was going through didn't seem fair. He was the person who I loved more than anyone in the world. I wished there was some way that I could have taken his pain and suffering myself so that he could be freed from this bondage. My tears flowed faster and my heart felt as if it were on the brink of exploding. I couldn't lay there any longer pretending that I was asleep, pretending that I didn't hear the pain he had tried so hard to hide from his children.

I wiped my red, swollen eyes and walked across the hallway into his room. He was surprised to see me there. "What's wrong dad?" I asked a question I already knew the answer to, but I didn't know what else to say.

"My foot is hurting pretty bad right now," he said while wiping his eyes. It was as if my acknowledgment of the elephant in the room finally gave him permission to honestly share what he was struggling with. He told me that the sore on his foot wasn't getting better. It was getting worse. The hole continued to get bigger. And, he said as his tears began again, the doctors were saying they would probably need to cut off his foot. Maybe some of his leg. Then he confided that the same problem was starting on his other foot. He was absolutely petrified at the thought of losing both his legs.

My fourteenth birthday was only days away, and I knew he would have given anything to go out to the driveway and play basketball together, as we did almost every night before he got sick. At that moment I came to the realization that not only would he be unable to play basketball with me on my birthday, but he may never be able to play basketball ever again.

As I tried to process what he was telling me, he looked up and smiled. "You're a good kid. I've got the best kids in the whole world. I love you guys so much. Go to bed now. Things will work out." I walked over to the bed and gave him a hug. It was a long, deep, lasting hug. It was the kind of hug that you feel in the very depth of your soul. At that time I didn't realize that this hug was one I would never forget. Despite the intense sorrow I felt, I also recognized how fortunate I was to be able to say this man was my father.

* * *

Days later my fourteenth birthday came and went. With his health in shambles, my father was no longer able to work. Often he would be there when I came home from school, but many times he was gone at doctor appointments.

I arrived home from school on a brisk January afternoon. Snow had fallen earlier in the day and a thin blanket of white covered the driveway. A soft crunch accompanied every step as I walked across the driveway and into the empty house. On the kitchen counter I saw a note my dad had written to us kids. He thanked us for all our help around the house since he wasn't able to do much. He said he appreciated us and gave us permission to take a day off from doing our chores. I happily walked to my room and flipped on my stereo. I sat on my bed while bad 80s music filled my ears.

A few minutes later I heard a loud scraping sound outside. In my mind's eye, I can recall the scene as vividly now as the moment it happened. I looked out the window to see my younger brother Kenny shoveling snow off the driveway. The thick metal of the shovel hammered at the cement as he tried to chip hardened pieces of ice off the driveway.

Then suddenly a loud scream pierced the cold, biting January air. More screaming. Kenny ran into the house. I was puzzled and couldn't understand why he would be yelling so loudly. I ran out of my room as Kenny came up the stairs. "The garage. The garage," he said through heaving gasps.

Time instantly began flowing in slow motion. Every second was slow, labored, and heavy. I ran out to the garage, which had been closed when we got home from school. It was now opened with the snow shovel laying across the driveway.

I looked to the side of the garage and saw a slumped foot wrapped in an Ace bandage. In dragging slow motion my eyes moved upward. Pants. Coat. Hands. The slumped body of my father next to the wall with a rope around his neck.

I ran out of the garage into the biting winter afternoon. But I didn't feel the cold wind. As I stood there on the driveway, I felt utterly swallowed by shock and sadness. I felt a hollow emptiness and gripping loneliness.

On that January afternoon, I was taught a lesson I never wanted to learn. I received an education no one is given in school. I was forced to learn to be strong and brave and compassionate.

On that January afternoon when I was fourteen years old, I learned how to suffer.

4) The Opposite Of A Natural Born Runner

High school track, marriage, and a desire to run a marathon

My brother Kenny, my sister Hollie, and I went through an understandable adjustment phase afterward. Adjusting to teachers pulling us out of class at school to say, "I'm just so sorry." Adjusting to life without dad. Adjusting to living with mom. Adjusting to a new neighborhood after we moved to a new house.

Aside from adjusting to the death of my dad, the following years were unremarkably similar to the lives of average teenagers. I went on Scout campouts. I worked as a bagger at the local grocery store. I played basketball after school with my friends.

I don't have one of those stories where I grew up loving to run. I didn't start running while I was young, progress to a triumphant high school and collegiate running career, win some marathons, and blossom into an elite ultramarathon runner. The only accurate part of this paragraph was that I grew up.

The extent of my running experience during youth happened in tenth grade. I suppose it would be safe to say that my high school running career (or dramatic lack thereof) began in the most unsuspecting location ever: history class.

I came to my seat one afternoon and a new student was sitting in the desk next to me, which had previously been empty. She had long brown hair and wore a green shirt and green earrings. She sat quietly in that awkward environment many new students experience when they change schools, feeling alone in a crowd where everyone knows everyone.

My friends and I all sat by each other. They introduced themselves, so I did, too. I found out her name was Melanie. The rest of the class session was spent with the teacher talking about Hiroshima and war. At least I think so. For all I know, the teacher could have been talking about the best technique to employ when trying to juggle four chainsaws, or explicit instructions on where to find buried treasure behind the school. I wasn't paying attention to a single thing the teacher was saying. I just kept thinking about Melanie.

A few weeks later, I heard from a friend of a friend that Melanie was planning to join the track team for the upcoming season. I wanted absolutely nothing to do with running. Running was punishment, not a sport. Running was torture, not a hobby. Running was miserable, not fun. But if Melanie was planning to join this miserable excuse for a sport, I may just reconsider.

Without having the slightest idea what I was getting myself into, I suddenly found myself wearing sweat pants that read "Jordan High School Beetdiggers" on the side. I'll pause for a moment while you consider whether the high school mascot of a "beetdigger" is a joke. (It's not.) Back in the early 1900s, when the school was built, it was surrounded by large fields of sugar beets. Vacation days were even allotted during harvest time for students to dig beets. Despite the fact that beet digging is now outdated, the school has proudly kept the mascot to maintain historical significance.

I found myself driving to the high school obscenely early in the morning when my body was telling me it wanted to be asleep. I found myself walking through the snow to a cold gymnasium, where it felt like the heater hadn't worked since World War II. I found myself doing stretches and drills and being barked at by football coaches who needed something to do during the offseason. I ran around the track. I hated every single solitary second of it. But I got to hate every single solitary second of it with Melanie.

One morning our coaches had us go to the weight room. I had no illusions about being able to get Melanie's attention or impress her with anything I could do in the weight room. The muscles in my arms are a nearly identical representation of the arms of Kermit The Frog. She laughed as my body shook while trying to do a pull up.

Despite my absolute lack of physical ability in the weight room or the track, we started talking more often. We started spending more time together. Though nothing formal had been decided, a relationship was growing.

In our time together, I learned that Melanie came from a large family with five other sisters. She said she wanted to be a nurse. (Since then she has followed all of her career plans, earning a nursing degree. She now works with hospice patients in a surgical assessment center, and in the Intensive Care Unit at the hospital in St. George, Utah.)

There were two options when I signed up for track: I could run sprints or I could run distance. I knew precisely nothing about running. I had no concept of distance or pace. I had no understanding of what it meant to run distance. I knew that running fast was hard. And I knew that if you ran distance, you could run slower. So I decided I'd run distance.

I went to the before-school workouts. I went to the after-school workouts. But my attendance had nothing to do with wanting to improve as a runner. I didn't run a single, solitary mile of training on my own during that track season. Not one.

Spoiler alert: Less-focused training results in some less-than-stellar track meets. I dreaded the track meets with other schools. They were evidence of how little training I had done and how much I hated running. Track meets were an embarrassment. I remember one meet in particular where I found myself running alone on the track while all the other runners were standing at the finish line already catching their breath. It would be interesting to look back on scores from the various track meets that year. I don't recall ever finishing any race better than last place.

My tenth-grade track season ended, and I resolved that unless I was being chased by someone with a chainsaw, I would never run again. By that point in time, running had led to something far more important to me than being a successful runner. Melanie was my girlfriend.

I knew our relationship was going the right direction when she said, "You have to stop calling me Melanie. Anyone who knows me well calls me Mel. Call me Mel." After a few more years of high school and then a year of college at Southern Utah University together, we were married.

I had never met a more selfless, compassionate, giving person. I admire how she is quick to laugh, quick to joke, quick to forgive, quick to smile, and quick to serve. She has an ability to make people feel important, and when she smiles, her face glows.

One night over dinner, I recalled that miserable high school track season. "Remember how I ran track that one year?"

"Yeah, why did you do that?" she asked. "You don't even like running."

"I know! I only ran it because you did!"

A look of shock and surprise crossed her face. Her eyebrows raised as she said, "You ran because I did? I ran because you did!"

In this moment of clarity we realized that neither of us wanted to run track. Both of us disliked running. Miscommunication between friends resulted in us both competing (a term I use very, very loosely) in a sport that we both wanted nothing to do with. And we both consented to run track because we both wanted to be with each other.

For years we lived the standard young, married college student life. We lived in a minuscule apartment. We were too poor to turn the heat on during the winter and walked around our shoebox-sized apartment with coats and mittens on to stay warm. We subsisted on a diet of Ramen noodles and Frosted Flakes.

I was accepted to graduate school in Wyoming to study social work. Our apartment in Wyoming was even smaller. Even more run down. Even colder. We didn't have a bed. We slept on an air mattress that we had to pump up every night before bed. Many mornings we would wake up laying on the floor because the air mattress had deflated during the night. Living a lifestyle like that either makes you love each other more, or it makes you kill each other. There were undoubtedly moments when we wanted to kill each other, but as time went by, we learned to love each other more.

After surviving two winters in Wyoming where the core of your body is constantly a solid block of ice, I graduated. We had come to love the small town of Laramie, but were eager to get back to Utah and be closer to family. We knew our bodies would need long-term thawing, and decided to move to southern Utah, where summer temperatures make a sauna feel cold.

I was reading the newspaper one morning in October. A bright picture covered nearly the entire front page of the newspaper. The picture showed thousands of runners on a road with the stunning red mountains of southern Utah in the background. I read all about the iconic St. George Marathon that happened the day before and felt something I never expected to feel about running: inspired.

I studied each picture. I read every article in that day's paper about the marathon. I could simply not fathom that a human being was capable of running 26.2 miles. I was inspired by the courage and determination that every one of those runners must have had.

As I sat at the kitchen table with the newspaper in my hand, a devil appeared on one shoulder and an angel on the other. The devil said, "Remember that time in tenth grade when the coaches had the team run three miles? Remember how horrible that was? Remember how you felt like a gorilla was standing on your chest?"

Then the angel whispered, "Yeah, but imagine how cool it would feel to *run a marathon!*"

The devil quickly piped up "Remember how you finished every race in last place? Remember what a bad runner you are?"

"Who cares how long it takes you to run 26.2 miles?" the angel said. "A marathon is a marathon, no matter how fast you run it. You should do it!"

For two weeks, that angel and that devil sat perched upon my shoulders and refused to stop talking. They both argued the same points over and over and over again. I could not get the images of marathon runners from the newspaper out of my head. After two weeks, the devil gave up his argument. The angel won. But I had an enormous fear about telling Mel my thoughts.

"She's going to laugh in your face!" I thought. "She's going to think you are playing a joke on her. She is going to remind you how much you despise running and how bad you are." I look back at these thoughts now and laugh that I was so nervous, but at the time I legitimately felt worried.

Finally one night, as we were sitting in bed, I worked up the courage to tell her my thoughts. I started talking with the same apprehension someone would feel confessing their sins to a priest.

"Mel, I've been thinking about something lately." She turned off the television and looked at me with a kind of concern that said, "Uh oh. This can't be good. He never talks about anything this seriously."

"I think I want to try running the St. George Marathon next year," I said.

I braced myself for mocking and ridicule. But instead of mocking she smiled and enthusiastically said, "Wow, really? Cool!" So with Mel's vote of confidence, I began training for my first marathon in the typical manner —spending hours glued to the computer while analyzing training plans.

I did everything the training plan told me to do. I was meticulous, rigid, and obedient. And, as countless runners before me and countless runners until the end of time will do, I was obedient to a fault. I listened much more closely to what the training plan told me instead of what my body was trying to tell me. A body takes time to adapt to the demands of running. But the training plan said to run two miles, so I ran two miles. When the training plan said to run three, I ran three. I was fifty shades of elated when I finished my first-ever five-mile run.

Meanwhile my legs were getting grumpier. My knees were achy and sore. I didn't listen to them. At the time, I didn't realize that being a stubborn, determined runner often leads to becoming an injured, sidelined runner. On a cold Saturday afternoon, I set out to run six miles for the first time. I completely ignored my legs, which were telling me to take some rest and delay the training plan for a while.

Halfway through the run, my knees buckled. It felt like someone dropped a filing cabinet from a ten-story building onto my knees. Not only was I unable to run, but even walking was painful. Those last three miles hobbling home were excruciating and I was overwhelmed with frustration.

I walked in the house and slammed the door before slumping onto the couch. Mel walked into the living room and said, "What's wrong?"

"That run sucked so bad. My knees hurt so bad. I can't run a marathon. I can't even run six miles! Six miles!" I said.

She left the room and I felt my dream of running a marathon evaporate into thin air. "I can't even run six miles," I muttered to myself. "Not even six miles." All the training plans I had printed went into the garbage, along with any intention I had of ever running again. The memories of thirteen years earlier as a sophomore on the track team and every miserable track meet flooded my mind. I couldn't believe I had been so foolish to even attempt training for a marathon.

Most of a year passed. I was eating my breakfast at the kitchen table on the first Sunday in October when I opened the newspaper and saw photos of the St. George Marathon, nearly identical from a year earlier. I tried to resist the rush of emotions. I tried to ignore the desire, hope and inspiration. But I just couldn't resist. I was immediately drawn to the stories of triumph and victory from all of the runners, whether they finished in first place or last place.

It was as though a video tape had been taken from a year earlier. I had the same conversation with Mel. "I think I want to try to run the marathon." I got the same response from her: "Great, go for it!"

I cut out marathon pictures from the newspaper and hung them up in my office at work so I could constantly be reminded of that inspiration. I printed the training plans. I started building my runs slowly. But yet again, I paid more attention to the training plan than to my body. I ignored cues to rest. And yet again, on what was to be my first six-mile run, I stood crippled with pain in my knees and feet halfway through. The exact same experience from the year before repeated itself. Training plans went in the garbage and I abandoned my desire to run. Just to make sure I didn't forget, my mind repeated over and over again: "You, Cory, are not a runner. You are not a runner."

5) Rubbing Curling Irons On My Legs

St. George Marathon 2009

The third year of taking the newspaper into Mel the day after the St. George Marathon deserved some skepticism. I wouldn't have blamed my wife one bit if she reprimanded me for even considering trying yet again to train for a marathon.

"I can't explain why," I said. "But for some reason I really, really want to go for this." I couldn't believe when her response lacked even the slightest degree of skepticism. She told me I could do whatever I wanted to do. "You can do this Cory. Go for it!"

And so with my annual marathon vote of confidence from my wife, I set back to preparing a training plan. I focused more than ever on learning from my past running mistakes. I listened to my body and rested when it told me to rest. As runners, we so often lack the self-control to back off when the body needs a break. The heart and soul of running is about pushing hard, being determined, and fighting through adversities. But I've come to realize that sometimes there is a price to be paid for pushing too hard and being too determined if we disregard the physical cues from our bodies.

On a monumental Saturday afternoon I managed to run six miles ... without hobbling home. It took a few years of trying, but I finally made it. Even after running hundred-mile races, I haven't forgotten the triumph I felt when I was able to run six miles. Every mile I was able to build onto my long run was a celebration.

I had been running for five months when I finally built up enough confidence to sign up for my first half marathon. I kept my pace under control the whole race and was overjoyed when I rounded a corner after thirteen miles and saw the finish line up ahead. As I neared the finish line a roar of cheering erupted from the spectators at the finish line. I swelled with pride as I thought, "Wow, what a great sport this is! It's so awesome that this huge crowd of people is cheering on my amazing athletic achievement!" Approximately three seconds later, I realized what the crowd was actually cheering about when an eleven-year-old boy darted past me right before I crossed the finish line.

When I started my quest to run a marathon, finishing was my only goal. I'd been diligent with my training and noticed that my endurance and speed were slowly increasing. Then somewhere along the way I changed my goal from "Run a marathon" to "Run a marathon … fast." Fortunately a few months before the marathon, a lightbulb went off during a training run. I realized that I was focusing so much on speed that it was taking a little bit of the fun out of running.

I wanted to make sure I would enjoy the whole experience of running a marathon. I didn't want to reach the finish line so exhausted that I didn't enjoy the journey. I wanted to suck everything I could out of the marathon, and if I was going to do that, I realized that I might have to slow down a little bit. I decided I would bring a little pocket camera with me during the race. It was possible that this would be the only marathon I'd ever run, and if it was, I wanted to remember every good, bad, and ugly detail of it.

* * *

The piercing sound of the alarm clock started chirping at 3:15 a.m. That sharp noise signaled the morning of my first marathon. I tried to wipe the four hours of sleep out of my eyes as I stumbled to the bathroom to get dressed. Lubrication on the feet: check. Band-Aids on the nipples: check. A penetrating terror that made my legs quiver: check. I met some friends at the location where runners boarded busses to the starting line. Nervous chatter filled the bus. Behind me, a girl was talking about how she accidentally pooped her pants during her first marathon. I thought in horror, "Oh no! What have I gotten myself into? I don't want to poop my pants. I don't want to poop my pants! Maybe I need to get off the bus right this instant." I sat on the stiff, green seat while the scent of BenGay assaulted my nose from all different directions of the bus.

After nearly a year of training and one long bus ride, I found myself standing at the start line of the St. George Marathon. At that moment, even making it to the start line felt like a victory. I carried my camera in an imitation leather fanny pack that I had purchased from the local thrift shop. It smelled like secondhand smoke and bounced up and down my waist when I ran. And then there was that minor detail that fanny packs had gone out of style a few decades earlier. I didn't care.

Within the first seven miles, I realized that "enjoying every second of the marathon" was far too lofty a goal. I stopped enjoying every second when I reached the dreaded Veyo Hill. In St. George Marathon lore, Veyo Hill strikes fear in heart of every runner it has chewed up and spit out. Unless your last name is Seabiscuit, chances are that Veyo will bring you to a walk (if it doesn't bring you to your knees first).

My plan was to follow the four-hour pace group. The group leader was smart, experienced, and knew way more about the whole marathon pacing thing than I did. I figured if I just stuck with him, my race would go perfectly. When we reached aid stations, I would stop momentarily, just long enough to grab and drink a cup of water. But each time I looked up after my drink, I would see the balloons of the four-hour pacer far ahead. So I sprinted to catch up and would stay with him until the next aid station, when the exact same thing would happen.

After fifteen miles, I realized this wasn't going to work. I needed to run my own race. But by then, it was too late. My foolish pacing early on would come back to bite me. I now found myself in the middle of the race dehydrated and worn out from going too fast to keep up with the pacer. I had committed the first cardinal sin of marathon running: going out too fast. (At least Band-Aids were preventing the second cardinal sin of getting bloody nipples.)

A few miles later, I passed my grandparents, who were standing on the side of the street cheering and waiting to see me in the midst of running my first marathon. They were so excited when I spotted them and stopped to say hello. With his typical sense of humor, my grandpa yelled, "Keep going! You are in first place! You are in first place!" completely disregarding the sea of runners stretched out ahead of me.

With seven miles left in the race, I suddenly felt a dog bite into my calf. I quickly turned around to see what rabid creature had sunk its teeth into my leg, but there was no animal. Instantly, another imaginary dog bit my other calf. A light bulb went off in my mind. "Oh no! This must be what leg cramps feel like." I had never experienced the kind of leg cramps that hurt so badly that they made me sick to my stomach. My muscles became as hard as baseballs as every muscle fiber in my legs tightened up. I tried stretching, but that only made them spasm worse. I tried rubbing them, but it felt like rubbing hot curling irons on my legs. Nothing helped. I then became a billboard for the term "Marathon Death Shuffle".

Consider this little nugget of wisdom by Tim Noakes from the book "Lore Of Running": it takes four to eight weeks to prepare mentally for a marathon "because the degree of discomfort experienced after eighteen miles in the marathon is the worst that most men, and most women outside of childbirth, ever experience. In order to cope with this, the mind needs to fully understand why it should drive the body through that pain barrier."

Wait. What? This could be the worst discomfort I would experience … and I paid for this? In that moment of agony where my legs felt like they were being shredded by cheese graters, I realized that Tim Noakes' quote wasn't just a cute saying. The guy knows what he is talking about.

A hefty dose of hobbling was involved to cover those last seven miles. With three blocks to go in the race, I saw the finish line ahead of me. I tried every ounce of strength and determination to free my legs from the marathon death shuffle, but my muscles remained twisted in knots. I fought the urge to punch a spectator in the throat after he called out, "Just run it, you're so close!" I remembered that I have Kermit The Frog arms, and I couldn't outrun the guy if by chance my fist made contact with his neck. So I ignored his well-intentioned but unhelpful encouragement and continued shuffling closer to the finish line.

After hours of running, miles of shuffling, sweat, tears, and legs that morphed into baseballs, I crossed the finish line of my first marathon. I was overcome with joy after accomplishing a goal that had been years in the making. In that moment, my life changed. Running had become a part of me. That moment was the beginning of so many amazing experiences that have come into my life because I am a runner. I can't begin to imagine how different my life would have been if I had given up on running after my first two failed marathon training attempts. I didn't recognize it years beforehand, but I actually was capable of running a marathon. How much are each of us capable of that we just don't realize yet?

6) My Mother-In-Law's Meatloaf

The first time my running shoes met dirt

M y friend Tom Dansie had finished the St. George Marathon with enough time that he could have gone home, showered, gotten dressed, eaten lunch, and taken a catnap by the time I finished the marathon. So you can imagine my concern when, four months after the marathon, Tom asked if I wanted to go on a trail run with him.

"Well, it sounds fun, but I've never been on a trail run before," I said. What I really meant when I told him it "sounded fun" was that it sounded scary. And intimidating. And hard. And not at all fun. My closing argument was, "I can't keep up with you for two minutes, let alone a whole run."

Tom tried to reassure me the way firefighters would reassure someone at the top floor of a burning house by telling them, "Don't worry, you can jump. We'll catch you." Tom said, "Don't worry, you can go as fast or slow as you want."

I made him promise that he would not feel obligated to stay with me. He could run ahead and I would catch up later. He agreed. So we shuttled our cars, leaving one at the end of the trail so we could drive back to the start when we finished. "I'll take you to one of my favorites. It's called the JEM Trail."

After time has passed, you can look back on experiences that, at the time, seemed mundane and inconsequential. But with time comes understanding. Even though you may not know it at the time, every once in a while you have those moments that end up shaping the person you become. This was one of those moments.

Tom's pace was much slower than he was used to for those first few miles we ran together. He ignored the fact that I was covered with sweat and nearly gasping for air while he floated effortlessly down the trail without the slightest hint of perspiration. I begged him to go on ahead and free himself from the shackles that were my cement legs. Finally he consented. Before parting he gave me some instructions about where to turn at upcoming sections of the trail. I pretended to understand, but in my mind I was thinking, "I don't understand a solitary thing he is saying. He might as well be giving me directions on how to run to Beijing."

Luckily for me, it's nearly impossible to get lost on the JEM Trail. At the one trail junction, Tom had spelled my name with pebbles, then used sticks to make an arrow pointing which way to go. (I was well aware of the fact that Tom had moved so far ahead of me over the course of three miles that he had time to craft an elaborate sign on the trail for me.)

While running, I was smitten by the beauty that surrounded me. I loved the challenge, the scenery, and the fact that I didn't see another person the entire time. I didn't know it at the time, but a fascination and love for trail running began to seep into my blood on that run.

I met Tom at the end of the trail, where we had a car waiting. I couldn't bring myself to ask him how long he had been waiting, though he didn't seem the slightest bit annoyed or impatient. We drove together back to the start, where he left his car. I remember our conversation as vividly as if it were yesterday.

"That trail run was so, so fun!" I said. We talked about how we had heard of trail races called ultramarathons, where people ran a hundred miles. We talked about how incredibly difficult it was to comprehend how this was even possible.

"I felt completely demolished after the marathon," I said. "I can't believe it is humanly possible to go another seventy-four miles." If, at that moment, a fortune teller told me "In a few years you'll be running one of those hundred-milers," I would have told them they were crazy. I would have emphasized that I was more likely to give birth to a baby giraffe named Penelope than to ever run a hundred miles.

From that very first run with Tom, I have fallen head over heels, madly in love with being on trails. I start to get the shakes like a junkie who has gone without a hit for too long when I don't get my trail fix every few days.

* * *

My mother-in-law makes some positively amazing meatloaf. I don't know what's in it and I don't want to know. I like the mystery. (I can only assume that ingredients include a mixture of sunshine, rainbows, and unicorn sparkles.)

Trail running is the same way. There are lots of little mysterious elements that make it seriously wonderful. Allow me to transform myself into Julia Child and expound on three ingredients that make meatloaf — I mean trail running — so awesome.

Ingredient #1 – The Scenery

Sure, you can see some beautiful stuff running on the road. Those parked cars and miles of endless white line on asphalt are nice to look at. But there is nothing that can match the beauty of a trail weaving through the aspens or cresting the top of a mesa, where you can see the expanse of nature surrounding you.

Ingredient #2 – The Uncertainty

Unlike the safe predictability of road running, you never quite know what you're going to get out on the trail. My mom's meatloaf is not very good. And by "not very good," I mean if you gave me the choice between eating a rusty radiator and my mom's meatloaf, I'd choose the radiator. (I'm sorry mom. But you always taught us to be honest.)

The point is that sometimes your experience on the trail can be as bad as an episode of "Golden Girls." Maybe you'll get lost. Maybe you'll trip and scrape your knees. But maybe you'll have that special run that is a magically delicious experience. (I just revealed my affection for Lucky Charms cereal.) I love that feeling of knowing that every run can be an adventure.

Ingredient #3 – The People

Runners are awesome people. Runners are family. But I experienced a new level of amazing when I got into trail and ultra running. For example, my friend Christie Ebenroth was running her first hundred-miler, and was crippled with horrible blisters. I saw a picture of her sitting on the side of the trail with her socks off. In the picture there was a guy who was helping clean her feet, bandage the blisters, and get her back on her way. This guy wasn't a family member. He wasn't an aid station worker. He was another runner. In the middle of his own race. And he stopped to help someone in need. That gives me goosebumps.

There is a vast difference between road races and trail races. When I am running a marathon, I don't need to carry too many provisions because I'll be hitting an aid station every two miles. If I get thirsty, it's not a big deal because I'll be at an aid station soon. But in trail and ultra races, it's not unusual for aid stations to be ten miles apart. And those ten miles can include river crossings, going up or down steep mountains, or long stretches through a hot desert. Instead of considering how to get to the next aid station twenty minutes away in a marathon, I have to think about precisely what I'll need to get me through another three (or more) *hours* of potentially brutal terrain.

I love the sport of trail running. And I love good meatloaf.

7) That Time I Swallowed A Gremlin

Stories from the span of 13.1 to 26 miles

had fallen head-over-heels for running. I loved the whole race environment. I loved the nervousness the night before a race while wondering what kind of adventures were in store. I peppered my regular running schedule with a hefty dose of miles on trails, but stuck to running half marathons and marathons on the road.

In 2010, I was so excited to run my second marathon in Ogden, Utah. Unfortunately four crucial errors took place in the week leading up to the race:

1) I invited bad karma by trying to avoid getting sick and invoking a strict No Kissing Policy with everyone in the house for the week leading up to the race. Sorry kids. Instead of the hug and kiss when I tuck you into bed, I'll give you an extra tight squeeze but no germ-transmitting kisses.

2) My six-year-old daughter Kylee begged to go on a date to McDonald's. I'm never one to turn down a date with a kid so we went. And I accidentally ate a large Big Mac combo meal. Oops.

3) The aforementioned six-year-old started barfing. I panicked.

4) Then, the day before the race it hit me. I'm not sure exactly what IT was. Food poisoning? The flu? Bubonic Plague? I don't know what it was, but it hit hard.

I knew I was in trouble when it felt like I swallowed a Gremlin. Then the Gremlin became angry and tried to claw its way out of my body. I couldn't eat or drink anything, or else I would upchuck. I felt so sick that I almost didn't make the five-hour drive up to northern Utah.

Still, I ended up making the drive. I had a sliver of hope that I would start feeling better, but the night before the race, I still felt disgusting. I knew, based on how I was feeling, that a marathon was out of the question. My whole body had that yucky, weak, achy feeling. At that point I wasn't discouraged about not being able to run the marathon. When you're praying for a visit from the Grim Reaper, a marathon is the least of your concerns. I managed to run the half marathon instead.

* * *

Mel decided to run her first St. George Marathon in 2010. We planned to run the whole race together. The bus ride to the marathon start line was full of the usual amount of nervous chatter, anxiety, and the suffocating smell of BenGay. Before the bus started, the driver told us where the exits were, how to locate a fire extinguisher, and where the emergency brake was in case she wasn't able to stop the bus. One witty runner said, "You haven't told us what to do in case of a water landing."

Just a few minutes before the start time, the lines for the portable toilets seemed at least a half marathon long. Consequently, lots of runners headed for the hills, bushes, and trees in the dark for a last-minute bathroom break. Mel decided she'd head for a bush, too. A few minutes later, I could smell her coming back. In fact, I could smell her before I could see her. She was distraught and said that in the darkness of the bushes she stepped in someone's poop! She did her best to wipe it off, but it still sloshed out the holes of her shoes when she stepped down. This is evidence of the fact that I love my wife: I still agreed to run with her for the next five-plus hours despite the smell.

Our friend Darrel tried to comfort her with a story of his own. He had waited in one of those thirteen-mile-long lines to get into a portable toilet. It was still dark outside, so when he sat down on the seat, he started sliding around. He then realized that the person before him didn't make it to the sitting position before having a bowel explosion. His backside was now covered in someone else's diarrhea. Suddenly Mel felt a little better about her predicament.

* * *

While on vacation in Mexico, we were laying on the beach when a street vendor who was selling wrestling masks passed. We politely said, "No thanks" — until I saw a Nacho Libre mask among the collection.

"Actually, I'll take one of those," I said. That mask sat in my closet for a few months until a thought crossed my mind. "I'm running the Utah Valley Half Marathon in a few weeks. And if there's one thing the Utah Valley Half Marathon needs, it's Nacho Libre!"

The day before the race, I bought some tight kids shorts, then headed to the women's clothing section at Walmart to complete the outfit with a flesh-covered tank top, which I stuffed with a sweatshirt to look like a pot belly.

I learned a few valuable lessons while running the race as Nacho Libre:

1) Running thirteen miles in a wresting mask feels like running thirteen miles with a black garbage bag over your head.
2) Capes are really itchy and scratchy.
3) A sweat shirt tucked into your shirt will bounce around like crazy.
4) A few people will look at your lumpy stomach and ask in all seriousness, "Is that real, or do you have something stuffed in there?"
5) Did I mention that capes are insanely scratchy? One woman clearly hadn't seen the movie Nacho Libre before when she asked, "Are you a pregnant wrestler?"

8) You're Going To Have To Jump

Taking chances, being brave, and living life
to the fullest

had fallen down a rabbit hole called YouTube. You know, those times where you watch the "More Cowbell" clip from "Saturday Night Live," and it somehow leads to a video about the best way to tape your feet to prevent blisters, which leads to a video about a guy puking his guts out while running Badwater, to a video about ... huh? Family Feud? My tumble down the YouTube rabbit hole left me sitting in front of my computer watching Family Feud host Steve Harvey talk to the audience after the show. I was surprised to hear Harvey talking about, of all subjects, taking risks.

I was immediately captivated by this candid moment with the audience when Harvey transformed from a comedian into the world's most inspirational speaker. "Eventually, you're going to have to jump," he said. "The only way for you to soar, is you've got to jump." With the conviction of a church preacher, Harvey talked about standing on the edge of a cliff. To go after the life we want, we have to take a chance. We have to jump!

He talked about how your parachute isn't going to open right away when you jump off that cliff. You're going to hit some rocks along the way. You're going to get some cuts and scrapes. His speech resonated with me as he spoke about how we could choose to play it safe, avoid the cuts and scrapes, and just stay on the edge of the cliff. If we do that, our parachute will never open. We'll never experience the depth of life's adventures. "You're gonna have to jump!"

Running has introduced me to countless people who have jumped off the proverbial cliff of life, and then proceeded to soar. They strive to live their lives to the fullest, and by doing so, inspire others to be brave and jump. One of those people who made the leap is Chris Praetzel.

I got a phone call one afternoon from Dixie Madsen, a friend I knew through work. She worked at Intermountain Donor Services, a nonprofit organization that coordinates organ transplants in our area. Working in a dialysis center, I had dialysis patients who worked directly with them to receive kidney transplants.

"Hey, there's a guy named Chris who is running across the country to raise awareness about organ donation," Dixie said. "His brother is only alive because of a kidney transplant. He's passing through southern

Utah tomorrow so I thought maybe you'd want to meet up with him for a few miles."

She gave me his email, and we coordinated a gas station to meet Chris the following night. I didn't quite know what to expect. I didn't know what kind of support crew Chris had or his route for passing through the area. We agreed to meet in the evening. It was June, when daytime temperatures regularly soar above a hundred degrees, so Chris was doing his running at night, then resting during the day.

I planned to park at the gas station, run with Chris for an hour, then turn around and run back to my car to go home. The thermometer in my car showed exactly one-hundred degrees when I pulled up to the gas station at 8 p.m. I was surprised to see a jogging stroller out front loaded with a backpack, cooler, and sleeping bag.

"No way," I thought. "He's doing this solo!" Then a guy walked out of the gas station who looked like he may be my twin brother. He was wearing running clothes and running shoes, and a smile spread across his face.

"Hey, are you Cory?" he said.

"Yeah, hi Chris! Wow, are you doing this thing solo?"

He confirmed that this cross-country trek was indeed a solo, self-supported adventure. We started running down the road as I asked question after question about his journey. I learned that Chris was running from California to New Jersey, where he was from. He had already traveled more than five-hundred miles, refilling his food and water supply each time he passed through a city or town. He slept at parks or behind churches most of the time. Basically, he slept wherever he could find a patch of grass to lay his sleeping bag where it wouldn't bother anyone.

Before arriving in southern Utah, Chris had passed through the Mojave Desert on one of the most barren, inhospitable, searing hot roads in the nation.

"I got stopped by the Highway Patrol a few times," he said. "They were getting reports from drivers that some crazy guy was running through the middle of the desert with a baby in a stroller." Once the Highway Patrol caught up with Chris and found out about his cause (and the minor detail that he didn't actually have a baby in his stroller), they were completely supportive. One member of the Highway Patrol even gave him a hat.

What I really admired was his determination, humility, and kindness. He told story after story after story about people who had reached out to help him along the way. Instead of seeing a cold, uncaring world, Chris saw the kindness and support of strangers.

After an hour of running with Chris, I turned around. The whole way back, I thought about his quiet modesty. Once I arrived back at my car, I called Mel and said, "Hey, this guy is amazing. He's really doing something amazing. He's going to be passing through Hurricane in a few hours. Chris didn't ask for one single thing, but what do you think about renting a cheap motel room for him tonight so he can have a shower and actual bed to sleep on?"

Being the compassionate soul she is, Mel didn't hesitate. "Sure!"

I picked up some food for Chris, then drove down the road to meet him. He was overwhelmingly appreciative and thankful for the food. I said, "You're going to pass through Hurricane in a few hours. We want to rent a room for you tonight. I'm going to drive ahead and get a room, then I'll come back and drop the key off for you."

He protested. "No, really, you don't need to do that for me." But the plan had already been set in motion.

I ran into a problem. I walked into the first motel and asked to rent a room for the night. "Sorry, we're sold out tonight," the clerk said. I drove to the next motel and got the same response.

"The motels around here are hardly ever all sold out," I thought. But when I got to the third and last motel, it was sold out as well.

I called Mel back. "You aren't going to believe this. Every room in town is sold out!" We decided we'd take our chances, hope that Chris wasn't an ax murderer, and offer to let him stay in a spare room at our house for the night. He seemed filled with gratitude when I drove back and explained that there weren't any motel rooms available, but he was welcome to stay at our house if he'd like.

I told him he could just rest or sleep during the following day, and then he could start running again in the evening when it cooled down.

He agreed. Chris slept well that night (and didn't murder our family with an ax.) The next day he said he'd like to come to church with us. Afterward we had dinner and Mel did her best to stuff him with as many calories as his skinny body would hold. He talked to my kids like an older brother who just arrived home from college on spring break. He told them stories and listened intently to all the stories they had to tell him.

As the sun began to set, Chris stood on the front porch with my family. He told us that if we were ever in New Jersey, we had a place to stay. He shook all our hands, thanked us for the stay, and then started running across the street. Across the neighborhood. Across the state. Across the country.

I found out later that my daughter gave him a note right before he left that read, "Dear Chris, my name is Danica and I believe that you will be able to finish your race. I'm glad that you were able to stay with us. I am so sorry that you won't be able to sleep on a nice comfy bed like you did at our house last night. Thank you so much for caring so much about your brother and running so long for him. I hope you will keep this note as long as you live. From Danica."

After four months and 3,330 miles, Chris arrived in New Jersey. He ran across the country. When Steve Harvey talked about experiencing life to the fullest and proclaimed, "You're gonna have to jump," he might as well have been talking about Chris.

The combination of life experiences with my father, working with chronically ill patients, and the lessons I've learned through running have all inspired my desire to jump. I fear living a life similar to the movie "Groundhog Day," where I wake up in the morning, work from eight to five, come home and watch television for a few hours, then go to bed, only to wake up the next day and do the same thing. Day after day. Month after month. Year after year. I don't want to look back on my year and see nothing but a long string of eight to fives. I want to jump!

* * *

While "You're gonna have to jump" is more of a metaphor for life, I've maximized jumping in a literal sense as well. In January 2011, I had an article published in "Runner's World Online" where I explained that I had only two goals in my running career. They were:

1) Run a marathon under four hours. I was confident that this would happen — when every planet in our solar system aligns, there was a sixty-three-mile-per-hour tailwind, and I could pick up a scooter at mile twenty.
2) Get a mid-race jumping picture.

Jumping pictures back then weren't what they are today. I had never seen a mid-race jump shot before. In the article, I wrote about how complicated this undertaking was. First, you have to spot the photographer far enough in advance that you can muster the strength to jump. Then you have to time the jump perfectly. You need to be airborne at the exact moment the photographer happens to snap the picture.

I wrote about having a chance to capture an epic jumping picture at the finish line of the Mesquite Marathon. A photographer was there, so I made an attempt at my first-ever jumping picture. I took a big leap into the air and prayed that the photographer had good timing. Considering that I had never done this before, I didn't know what to expect at the landing. I momentarily forgot that I had just run 26.2 miles. When my feet returned to Earth, my legs buckled and I nearly earned myself a mouth full of pavement. I heard a few disapproving comments from people who said, "You know, you should be more careful. You probably shouldn't be jumping after a marathon." Of course their comments didn't make me want to stop jumping, but instead made me want to get better at it.

When the pictures came out, the jump shot was a fail. The camera clicked right as I landed and my face looked like someone had just stabbed a number-two pencil in my spleen. Fortunately, a few months later, I ran the St. George Half Marathon and took another crack at a jumping picture. This time it worked. I got a full, mid-air jumping jack picture at the finish line.

After that "Runners World" article about jumping pictures, my blog at www.fastcory.com took off. I've continued taking jumping pictures while running races or in scenic locations ever since.

When I take a jumping picture, it's to show how much fun running can be. Our sport isn't all about suffering and pushing the limit and going hard. If you're going to stick with running for life, it better be fun. It's impossible to be unhappy while taking a jumping picture!

"Those who don't jump will never fly." ~ Leena Ahmad Almashat

9) I'm Sorry To Tell You This, But They're Both Broken

An impromptu ultramarathon, 2011

O ver the next year, I ran a chunk of half marathons and marathons, but my training was transitioning more and more to trails. I was eager to try a trail race, but it seemed like almost all trail races in my area were ultramarathons.

One day while out on a trail I had an epiphany. "Wait. I love spending all day running through the wilderness. And that's exactly what an ultramarathon is: an all-day run through the wilderness with an aid station every hour or two!" I set out to find a race that would be a good fit for a first ultra.

In April 2011, I ran my first fifty-kilometer race (thirty-one miles), the Red Mountain 50K in southern Utah. Red Mountain was a logical choice, because it was a local race. I'm sure it was my nerves, but the bus ride to the starting line seemed to take forever. Honestly. I felt like I could have watched the whole "Hunger Games" movie series during that bus ride. When we got off the bus, it was freezing outside with a brisk wind. After about two minutes of standing out in the cold, we got right back on the bus and waited until it was time to start.

Once the race started, I felt right at home on the trails. A few minutes after I passed the aid station at mile nine, I reached a river. I thought, "Hmm. That's strange. I don't remember a river in the course description." The reality was that I hadn't studied the course too closely leading up to the race, so I chalked the river up as something I had simply overlooked. The only runner I had seen for a few miles was a guy a quarter mile ahead of me. When he reached the river he charged right through it. There was the option to leave a change of shoes for the mile twelve aid station, when the trail portion of the race ended and the remaining miles were on roads. But I chose not to leave a change of shoes because I didn't know we'd be crossing a big river. I walked up the river to search for a shorter distance to cross, but found no options. No luck going down river either. I didn't want to run through it and have wet shoes for the next twenty-two miles so I sat down, took my shoes off, and waded to the other side.

After I put my shoes on again, I started running up a steep hill. I had run a mile past the river when I thought I saw a group of around fifteen runners charging toward me. I figured it was too early in the race to start hallucinating. Apparently they had gone farther up the trail, hadn't seen any course markings, and realized they had gone the wrong way.

We ran a mile back to the river and had a pow wow about what to do. Someone concluded that we took a wrong turn and needed to go back across the river! So I took off my shoes AGAIN and waded back to the other side. Apparently a prankster sabotaged the course by changing the direction of the arrows. Standing at that river again with everyone deliberating about where to go was the craziest thing I had ever seen during a race. (I laugh to think about the number of times similar things have happened to me in races since then. Anyone who has run an ultramarathon can attest that it's not at all unusual to accrue some bonus miles along the way.)

* * *

The ultrarunning bug had bitten, and I was eager to try bumping up my distance. I'd heard about the Antelope Island Buffalo Run and decided I would try tackling the fifty-mile race.

Antelope Island is in the middle of the Great Salt Lake in northern Utah. The island happens to be home to a large herd of buffaloes, hence the race name "Buffalo Run." I trained diligently for the race. Having a base of marathons helped me build my mileage more easily.

Two weeks before the race, I was out on a ten-mile run. I had arrived at a point in my training where ten miles wasn't difficult and I could recover quickly. I had what I now realize was a foolish thought, but at the time it seemed totally reasonable: "The race is coming up soon. My legs are feeling good and it's easy to run ten miles. There is a hundred-mile race on Antelope Island that starts the day before the fifty-miler. Maybe I could switch from the fifty-miler to the hundred-miler!"

I got home and emailed the race director to see if I could switch to the higher distance. He said that would be fine, so the plan was set in motion. For the next week, I prepared drop bags, tried to figure out what I would do for nutrition, and had many restless nights with my mind trying to comprehend what it would take to run a hundred miles.

A few days before the race, I planned to work the first half of the day, then my family and I would make the drive to northern Utah. I was getting ready to leave when I received a call from Mel.

"Hello?" I said as I picked up the receiver. Between gasps and crying I heard "I fell ..." Then the phone clicked dead.

In a panic, I called back over and over again but there was no answer. I rushed out of my office to my car. After fifteen minutes of no answered calls that felt like an eternity, I called again. My mother-in-law answered the phone. "Mel fell pretty hard. I'm taking her to Instacare. Meet me over there."

When I arrived, Mel's eyes were sunken, surrounded by dark rings with tear-stained cheeks. She was about to be taken to the X-ray department.

"What happened?" I asked. She told me that she was in our bedroom when her feet got caught on the cord of an electric blanket. She tripped and was unable to catch herself before hitting the ground. Her elbows were X-rayed as she sobbed in pain. For the first time, I realized that my first hundred-mile ultramarathon may not happen.

We sat in a waiting room quietly contemplating this trial when the doctor walked in. "I'm sorry to tell you this, but both elbows are broken."

At that moment, for at least the short term, our lives changed drastically. The doctor decided to wrap her arms in bandages and slings instead of putting both arms in hard casts. Try to imagine what it would be like if even the slightest movement of your arms caused sheer agony. With two broken elbows, Mel could do absolutely nothing. She couldn't feed herself. She couldn't go to the bathroom by herself. She couldn't shower or get dressed or use the phone by herself. Not only did the pain make her cry, but so did her complete dependence on other people. She had tears in her eyes when she needed help with even the simplest of tasks. "Cory, could you scratch my nose?"

We went back and forth, seeming to vacillate by the minute, about whether or not I should attempt the race. I reluctantly came to the conclusion that it wouldn't be wise to try running a hundred miles if I needed to provide complete care for my wife and kids afterward. I felt heartbroken about my wife's injury and the pain she was in, as well as the thought that months of hard work and training would be wasted.

I found a sliver of consolation when I remembered that there was a new marathon being held three minutes away from home on the same day that I would have been running a hundred miles. My in-laws said they would babysit the kids (and my wife) if I wanted to run the marathon on Saturday, so I agreed.

I was sitting on the couch with Mel the evening before the marathon when a few friends sent me a text. Karrie Nielson and Cherie Santiago said, "If you want to run your first fifty-miler, you can run the marathon and then we will crew for you for the last twenty-four miles. My heart filled with gratitude for such caring, thoughtful friends. After they sent that text, I had an idea that hadn't crossed my mind before. "What if I started running tonight while Mel is sleeping and finish twenty-four miles before the marathon. Then the last twenty-six miles will be run with the actual marathon."

As she was with every crazy idea in the past, Mel was supportive. She stayed at her mother's house and I began my twenty-four mile run at midnight. Since the idea was so spontaneous, I didn't have any particular route in mind. I just pushed "start" on my Garmin watch and started running. I ran past houses, gas stations, and farms in my town. I watched as more and more lights in houses went dark with each passing hour. In the early morning, while the rest of the world slept, I was running. And at each moment, I thought about the experiences my wife and family had been through over the past few days. I wondered what our future would hold. I was oblivious to the quiet world around me as I was lost in thoughts.

I finished the first twenty-four miles with just enough time to change into clean clothes and grab some toast to eat before arriving at the starting line of the marathon. It was a first-year race, so the crowd was fairly small. Half way through the race, the sky opened up and dumped on us like a garden hose.

I finished the marathon in pouring rain with Mel waiting at the finish line. My son had finished a kids' run earlier in the morning, and was there as well. Every time I look at the picture of us together, I feel sad for everything Mel went through. Standing at the finish line with slings around each arm, she looked simply exhausted.

She had a few more days of being completely unable to do anything for herself before going into surgery to repair the damage. After her fall, I kept thinking I would wake up from this nightmare. "You will NOT believe the crazy dream I had last night!," I would tell Mel. "I dreamed that you fell. And you broke both of your elbows!" It was a harsh reality (infinitely more so for her) to realize that this wasn't a dream. I smiled at how happy she was after surgery, when she regained the ability to itch her own nose without asking someone for help. It was a stark reminder of the countless little things I take for granted each day.

Having run hundred-mile races since then, I can easily see that at that time I wasn't prepared to run one-hundred miles. I now see that being able to comfortably run ten miles and having a strong desire aren't enough to get you through a hundred miles. In all likelihood, Mel's fall prevented me from making a horrible mistake by trying to run a hundred miles while being unprepared. There would be plenty of opportunities in the future for mistakes to be made.

10) Intentional Suffering

Lessons from working with the chronically ill

When my kids were younger, we used to read the book "Selma" together all the time. The book is one of my all-time favorites. It's about a sheep named Selma who has the same routine every day. She wakes up, eats some grass, plays with her kids, chats with the neighbor, eats some more grass, and sleeps well at night.

When Selma is asked what she would do if she had a million dollars, she says that she would wake up in the morning, eat some grass, play with her kids, chat with the neighbor, eat some more grass, and have a good night's sleep.

When Selma is asked what she would do if she had more time, she responds that she would wake up in the morning, eat some grass, play with her kids, chat with the neighbor, eat some more grass, and have a good night's sleep. Selma is just plain happy with her life.

I feel exactly like Selma. I wake up in the morning, sometimes go for a run, spend the day at work, come home and spend some time with the family, tuck the kids into bed, then go to sleep. And the next day I wake up and do it all over again. I think I would choose to do the exact same thing if I had a million dollars or if I had more time. I feel so happy, so thankful.

My perspective on life changed in 2004. I had been working as a therapist at a residential teen treatment program. I absolutely adored working with the kids in my group. But an opportunity came up to start working as a medical social worker at some dialysis centers in the area. Dialysis is a medical procedure for people who have kidney failure. When people's kidneys no longer function adequately, they must have a dialysis treatment every other day to have toxins cleaned out of their blood. Once people start dialysis, it continues for the rest of their lives. Three or four-hour treatments, every other day, for the rest of their lives. No vacation from treatment. No holidays. No spontaneous trips to take the kids to Disneyland.

Often when people finish their dialysis treatment, they don't feel too great. They are tired and worn out. As a social worker at a dialysis center, I sit down and visit with patients during their dialysis treatments. They are sitting in their treatment chair with two needles in their arm attached to tubes. One tube carries blood out of their body to be cleaned by the machine, and another tube goes back into their arm to return the clean blood.

Every day at work, I am surrounded by people who are being bombarded with unintentional suffering. They have kidney failure and are faced with a life on dialysis. Some have cancer. Some are old and have to depend on others for everything. The thought of facing challenges like theirs scares me. A lot. They don't have a choice. There is no escape from their suffering.

One of the things that draws me so strongly to ultrarunning is the fact that it is chosen suffering. Even when I am the most miserable — when my legs are cramping like crazy, or when I'm dehydrated and sick, or when I'm so exhausted that I start talking to Smurfs — one thought keeps me going: I chose this! Nobody is making me do this. It is my choice.

All of those people drowning in unintentional suffering around me would love to be able to venture out onto a trail and try to run a hundred miles, even if it meant that they were cramping like crazy, dehydrated, exhausted, and talking to Smurfs. They would trade places with me in a heartbeat.

I started hearing a consistent theme in the patients I talked to: absolutely do not take your health for granted. Be spontaneous and take chances in life, because one day spontaneity could be taken away from you. If something is worth doing, do it now. Don't wait. You don't know what tomorrow will hold. Live life to the fullest each and every day. Live your life in a way that you won't look back with regrets, thinking about all the things you wish you would have done.

Since then, I have tried to let their encouragements guide my life. If there is a race I want to run, I'm going to run it now. If there is a goal I want to achieve, I want to start working toward it now. I want to avoid the possibility of looking back on life and seeing missed opportunities. I want to challenge myself and grow personally. I want to nurture the relationships that are important. I want to encourage and support and give to others. And I want to do it now.

11) I Barfed All Over My Shoes

My first hundred-mile race, 2011

In the months following Mel's double broken elbow extravaganza, I had a stirring interest to attempt a hundred-mile race. I browsed blogs, message boards, and Facebook groups, reading about various races. When I came across a hundred-mile race in Arizona called the Javelina Jundred, I had an instinctual feeling that this was the race for me. Javelina became my long-term goal, and I dedicated the rest of the year to race preparation.

The easy part of preparation included reading race reports, compiling lists of supplies I may need in drop bags, and scouring the internet for any morsel of information I could gather about running ultramarathons. I read about nutrition, hydration, and shoes. I read about blister treatment, training suggestions, and what to do if your stomach goes into complete revolt during a race and you can't stop barfing. I read about mental preparation, endurance, and tools to keep going when all you want to do is quit.

The hard part of preparation was actually implementing everything into my training. I'll speak more to the mental aspects of running (which are at least as important as the physical aspects of training) in a later chapter.

Using online training plans as a guide, I developed my own plan that would fit my schedule and hopefully leave me prepared for the race. I am unspeakably thankful for an employer who allows for a flexible work schedule. Generally I have a day off in the middle of the week, which allowed me to leave for a run after the kids went to school, run the entire day, and then arrive home around the same time the kids got home from school. This was a gigantic advantage that allowed me to train for ultramarathons while having minimal impact on family life.

On an average week, I would wake up early and run for an hour before work on Mondays and Tuesdays. On Wednesdays I would run all day, and be home in time to make dinner for the family. I would plan to run for an hour or two before work on Thursdays and Fridays, while giving myself flexibility to take a rest day if my body felt like I needed it. Saturday mornings, I would wake up early and run for three or four hours, often getting home before Mel and the kids woke up. Sundays were rest days.

The mid-week long run was cherished time to be out on the trails alone for the whole day. While many people get through the work week by looking forward to the weekends, I looked forward to my long run. With hundreds of miles of trails all within a short drive, I never got sick of running in the same places. And even on the trails that I regularly run, sometimes a few times a week, there is a sense of familiarity and love for my regular stomping grounds.

My long run was the opportunity to conduct science experiments, using my body as the guinea pig. Each week was approached with a question or a purpose. For example:

- I brought a variety of snacks and fruit to leave in my car, then stopped every five miles to see what sounded good to eat. I wanted to see what foods would sound appetizing after running in the heat all day.
- I ran with a full hydration pack as a backup, but tried to see how little water I could drink during a long run.
- I took salt tablets during one run, then compared how I felt by not taking salt tablets on the next run.
- I experimented with different ways of staying cool during hot runs, including putting ice in a hat, and ice in a bandana around my neck. (After countless miles of scorching heat during training and races, I've come to realize that wrapping ice in a bandana around my neck is the absolute gold standard for helping to keep cool during hot runs. The cooling effect borders on miraculous. Go ahead and try it. I promise you'll love it.)
- I had calories and nutrition available as a backup, but experimented to see how few calories I could get away with consuming during a long run. (By going slower, we're able to burn the nearly endless supply of fat our bodies all carry instead of solely relying on burning glycogen. Additionally, I've found that the later it gets in ultramarathons, the less enthusiastic my stomach is about taking in calories. I think it helped that I completed training runs without taking in any calories.)
- On some long runs, I experimented by consuming as many calories as I could. (Spoiler alert: This made me

nauseatingly sick … which also happens to be good
training for what is a common feeling late in races!)
- I tried different run/walk schedules to see how this
impacted my overall pace, and how my legs felt after a run.
- I tried various recovery techniques, including taking in
protein after runs, stretching, using a foam roller, and
taking ice baths (which happen to be pure, unadulterated
torture).

My focus in training was to have my body experience (on multiple
occasions) every possible complication or circumstance that may arise
during a race. Yet even with all this experimentation and preparation, I
still underestimated the difficulty of completing a hundred-mile race.

After many months of training, it was time to leave the familiar trails
of my hometown and put my preparation into practice. The day before
the race, Mel and I drove up the road to McDowell Mountain. My
stomach felt like it was overflowing with butterflies. We drove in silence
to the starting line of the race, where we would set up a tent for our race
headquarters. The towering saguaro cacti stood like sentinels lining the
road. Mel broke the silence when she looked over and said, "How are
you feeling?"

"Like I'm going to throw up," I muttered.

McDowell Mountain Regional Park lies on the outskirts of Phoenix,
Arizona. The arid desert landscape is fiery hot during the day and can be
frigid at night. McDowell is the staging ground of the Javelina Jundred,
named for the wild, and sometimes ferocious wild pigs called javelinas
that roam the wilderness.

I knew the Javelina Jundred would be a perfect opportunity for my
first hundred-mile attempt. The race's barren, rocky trails are very similar
to the trails I run near my home in southern Utah, so I felt right at home
on the course.

The Javelina Jundred course consists of a 15.4-mile loop run
washing-machine style, where runners finish a loop and then turn around
to head back around the loop in the opposite direction. The final blow of
the race is a shorter ten-mile loop that inevitably feels like it is seventy
miles. Javelina is known as a beginner-friendly race. The loop format

means that runners are never too far from an aid station, the trails aren't very technical or rocky, and there isn't a lot of elevation gain compared to other hundred-mile races. Despite these characteristics, I always cringe when I hear new ultramarathon runners choose the race because it is "an easy hundred-miler" — which is what I thought when I first registered for the race. At this point, having run many "easy" hundred-milers and many "hard" hundred milers, I can say with absolute certainty that there is no such thing as an "easy" hundred-miler. One hundred miles is one hundred miles, whether the trail goes upward or not.

The next morning I found myself standing at the starting line of my first hundred-mile race, suffocated by feelings of inadequacy and insecurity. Every single runner around me seemed so confident. So athletic. So brave. So very brave. And yet I stood there feeling completely alone in a crowd of runners. I felt so nervous. So nonathletic. So afraid. So very afraid. My mind was reeling with doubt. "Have I trained enough? How am I going to handle things when they start getting ugly? Do I really have what it takes to finish this thing?"

I was relieved to find that the moment the race started, those fears and insecurities immediately faded. My body seemed to realize that there was a job to do, and I wouldn't have any energy to waste on worry and fear. It would take every ounce of energy — and more — to find my way to the finish line.

I ran a handful of miles in the dark by the light of my headlamp. When the sun began to rise, temperatures soared. I reached that dreaded moment where it feels as though your skin is melting off your bones, and before you know it your skeleton will be standing in a pile of mush.

My energy level vacillated quickly between peaks and valleys. The quote — "Whether you're feeling good or bad during an ultramarathon, don't worry, it will pass" — is completely accurate. There was an experience that came back to haunt me at Javelina, and which I have tried to remember during every race since then. It happened during one of my high points around mile thirty-five. I was feeling good and maintaining a steady pace. I passed two runners, a young lady and an older man. As I passed, the man said in a reassuring tone quiet enough that it was only supposed to be heard by her ears, "Don't worry about people passing. The race doesn't start until mile seventy."

I thought that old man was crazy. I thought to myself, "What are you talking about? The race doesn't start at mile seventy. It started thirty-five miles ago and we're right in the middle of it." While I could understand how one may have the perspective to conserve until later in the race, it seemed more appropriate to take advantage of the times I felt good and run hard while those times lasted. (That mistaken thinking came back to bite me hard when I was at mile seventy and praying for a visit from the angel of death.)

The Javelina Jundred is held on the weekend closest to Halloween, so many runners dress up in costumes during the race. I remember a distinct moment when I truly fell in love with ultramarathons. It was late afternoon when I passed a runner who, fittingly, was dressed as a toilet. He was walking slowly and seemed to have a bit of a limp. As I passed, I asked "How are you doing?" — although judging by his gait, I already knew the answer.

He looked up at me and smiled as he said, "Good. Really good." But I could tell that his "good" sentiment wasn't a sassy, sarcastic remark. It was genuine! Despite the fact that he was feeling terrible, he actually was doing well because he was thankful to have the opportunity to be in the midst of a race, surrounded by beautiful scenery while testing the limits of his body. I realized the fact that optimism is prevalent, even rampant in ultramarathons. Runners can be having an absolutely miserable race and yet still be cognizant of the fact that they are undertaking something amazing.

I loved how the race was a series of loops. It was so fun to watch the race unfold and have the faster people come by going the other direction. I cheered for each of them as they passed. But what was awesome was that they were cheering for others as well. When the fast, elite runners would pass me, they would smile and say, "Great job!" or "Looking good!" It's quite the emotional boost to have elite runners give you a compliment like that.

The aid stations at the race were the best I had ever seen. I was used to aid stations at marathons, where the options were water, Gatorade, bananas, oranges, and occasionally a gel packet. Javelina was like a Saturday afternoon at Costco, where vendors are strewn throughout the store handing out samples. During the race I ate brownies, gummy worms, M&Ms, pretzels, pizza, a turkey sandwich, peanut butter and jelly sandwiches, Ramen noodles, oranges, bananas, watermelon, hot chocolate, pumpkin pie, and Oreos. And I didn't just have a little. Since my stomach was cooperating, I ate lots.

During the race I discovered two items sent straight from heaven: Nutella sandwiches and bean burritos. At each aid station I was popping those like a drug fiend. I know what you're thinking: "Bean burritos plus ultramarathon equals ultra-disaster." By the grace of God, those burritos never caused any problems. I expected a nuclear attack in my intestines, but it never came. (Thank goodness, because, whoa. *Whoa*. That could have gotten ugly.)

Years ago, I listened to an interview on Ultra Runner Podcast where the runner gave tips for running your first hundred-miler. One of the tips was to wait on listening to music from your iPod until the second half of the race. By then, you'll be so worn out and exhausted that the music will give you a nice boost. I took that advice. And by doing so, I learned a valuable lesson that hadn't been mentioned in the podcast: be very, very careful about what you let enter your ears before a race. Often, a song will get trapped in your head and set on repeat hour after hour after hour. That is wonderful if you're lucky enough to get a Bruce Springsteen song set on repeat in your mind. But somehow during the Javelina Jundred, I got the theme song from "The Facts Of Life" stuck in my head. "You take the good, you take the bad, you take them both and there you have the facts of life; the facts of life." Ahhhh! I have absolutely no idea how this song entered and began tumbling through my brain. Each repeat of the song was like stabbing an ice pick into my eardrum. And I couldn't make it stop!

My race changed after mile sixty. It started to sprinkle rain. Then the rain came down harder, until it turned to a complete downpour. The trails became slick and muddy, and much more difficult to run. In the previous months, Mel had been doing some running with the plan to pace some of the race. She came out to pace for fifteen miles during the worst weather.

My sister Hollie Doyle came to Arizona to crew, as well as get a taste of the ultramarathon atmosphere. Not only was she helpful in pacing for the next fifteen miles of the race, but she was also the self-appointed chief poster maker. My personal favorite was a large poster board covered with pictures of dancing Care Bears surrounding the words, "Hey Cory, let's chat!" Hollie is basically amazing.

Mel rejoined me for the last nine miles of the race. Even though I was happy to be on the last lap, I was a complete mess. I knew I would make it to the finish line, but I had absolutely no idea how. Every cell of my body was screaming. My gas tank was completely dry and I had nothing left to give.

Bob Glover said, "You'll be wistful for the 'wall' of the marathon when you hit the 'death grip' of the ultra." There is no amount of training that can prepare you for what the death grip of the ultra feels like. Imagine the feeling of being run over by a Greyhound Bus, then having vultures pick at the messy roadkill of Injinji socks and muscles knotted in charley horses. Then multiply that feeling by about nine billion. Now you're getting close.

I had heard that in an ultramarathon, you experience the highest of highs and the lowest of lows. For me, those things happened at the exact same time. And it was at mile ninety-five. I was only six miles away (the race was actually 101 miles), but that finish line might as well have been in Portugal. I started sobbing. Not loud weeping. I just silently walked as tears rushed down my face. Normally I'm not an emotional person, but at that moment my eyes were like faucets flowing with water.

I was crying because of the crippling pain. I was crying because of complete exhaustion and despair. I was crying because each step hurt worse than the one before it. I was crying because I so desperately wanted to be at that finish line. I was crying because I was so thankful for the body God gave me. I was crying because I thought of my family and friends and their tremendous support. I was crying because I was so thankful to be part of this incredible experience. I was crying because I knew that the last forty miles had been so indescribably difficult, and because of that, the finish line would feel even sweeter. I was crying because I was so, so happy.

Each step slowly moved me closer to the finish line. I laughed as I considered the fact that before the race, a six-miler was considered an easy morning run. But covering the last six miles of a hundred miler feels like an eternity. With one mile left to go, Mel grabbed my arm and said with fear, "Cory, look!" A few feet away, through my blurry vision, I saw an animal. Or maybe there wasn't anything there. Maybe it was a hallucination.

"It's a huge coyote," she said. I didn't have an ounce of energy left in my body to be scared. I think I had the same reaction to the coyote that I would have had whether it was a rabbit or a Tyrannosaurus Rex: a simple shrug of the shoulders and a slight raise of an eyebrow as if to say, "Huh, interesting." At that moment, I actually hoped the coyote was vicious and would eat me to put me out of my misery. I wasn't worried about my wife. She didn't need to outrun the coyote. She only needed to outrun me. (And I was moving at the speed of a kitchen table.)

Suddenly I crested the top of a hill and looked into the distance. I saw tents. I heard music. I saw the most beautiful thing my eyes had ever beheld (aside from my wife and kids of course.) The finish! My pace quickened and I was soon jumping across the finish line. When I crossed the finish line, someone handed me a belt buckle.

Hundred-mile races traditionally hand out belt buckles to finishers. Granted, someone could go to Walmart and purchase a belt buckle for $19.99. That's a heck of a lot cheaper than a race registration fee! Not to mention saving yourself the time and effort of training, and that minor detail of actually running a hundred miles. But when you cross the finish line of a hundred-miler, the belt buckle you are given is worth more than its weight in gold. The belt buckle is a symbol of hard work, dedication, perseverance, and determination. You have to be brave and courageous to earn a buckle. You must be a warrior to receive a buckle, and when someone puts that buckle in your hand, you will smile with the knowledge that you were willing to push yourself beyond the limits of body and mind.

I had a smile from ear to ear. As much as I couldn't have imagined the difficulty involved in running a hundred miles, I also couldn't adequately imagine the joy I would feel after such an accomplishment. As I was sitting at the finish line basking in pride, thinking that absolutely nothing could ruin how I was feeling, I unexpectedly swallowed down some barf that suddenly decided it wanted to erupt from my stomach.

When I tried to walk to the car, I had to quickly sit down because I got lightheaded and almost passed out. Admittedly, I was surprised how quickly my body shut down after the race. It was as though my body had this pact: "All right, I'll hold it together for you because you want this silly accomplishment of finishing a hundred miles. But the moment you cross that finish line, I'm clocking out for the day! You're on your own. I'm tired. Game over." When we arrived back at our condo after the race, I wasn't nearly as successful choking down my vomit. In fact, I got out of the car and ended up barfing all over my shoes.

And people call this fun.

In the days and weeks following the Javelina Jundred, I couldn't stop thinking about the race. At night I would dream that I was running down the trail, past towering saguaro cacti while sweat streaked down my face. In my sleep I could hear the coyotes howling in the distance like they did during the night of the race. Sometimes I would walk to my dresser where my belt buckle sat, just to touch it and see if it was real. I still couldn't believe that a human being was capable of moving forward nonstop for a hundred miles, and I certainly couldn't believe that of all human beings, *I* was capable of moving forward nonstop for a hundred miles.

The finish line of that hundred-miler changed me. I had confidence that I could do whatever I put my mind to. Reaching that finish line was a profound, challenging, painful, rewarding, and life-changing experience. Crossing that finish line transformed me.

12) I've Never Seen Breaking Bad

Balancing running and family

I live in the southern Utah town of Hurricane, population 15,000. Despite its spelling, our city is not pronounced the way you would pronounce the tropical storm. Locals pronounce the city "Hurr-kun." I have rebellious friends who, in an effort to "stick it to the man," pronounce Hurricane just how it is spelled. (That is a sure way to get a disapproving look from the locals.)

You'll find a few stop lights on your way through town, as well as the usual fast food chains, a hardware store, and some car washes along State Street. Everyone was thrilled when the town grew big enough to justify a Walmart.

What Hurricane is best known for is being a gateway to many national parks, and loads of tourists pass through on their way to Zion National Park, Bryce Canyon National Park, or the Grand Canyon. Hurricane also happens to be trail running's best kept secret. I maintain that this location is the mecca of trail running. People just don't know it yet.

Hurricane is a great place to raise kids. I would know. I have three offspring of my own. At the time of this book, Jackson is fifteen, Danica is thirteen, and Kylee is twelve years old. These little creatures are the spark plug of my life. We also have two dogs. The first is a big, black, fluffy poodle named Jack, and the second is a Great Dane we named Little Debbie.

Jackson is a piano virtuoso and can play Billy Joel's "Piano Man" so beautifully it will make you cry. He is also brutally honest. When I got home from work one day, I was joking with the kids about how Jack had just been groomed, and now he looked like a reindeer, so I started calling him Blitzen. Then I started joking about how Little Debbie was like a Shetland Pony. And then I started calling her My Little Pony. Then I sang the My Little Pony theme song over and over. I thought I was being hilarious ... as the kids stood there staring at me stone-faced. Finally, Jackson said, "Dad, you're not funny if nobody else is laughing." He has taken up CrossFit with Mel and now they speak CrossFit language together while the rest of us have no idea what they're talking about. (Push jerks? Thrusters? Kipping? Are you making these words up as you go along?)

Danica is also a piano-playing wizard, and can embarrass anyone who dares to challenge her at the video game "Just Dance." A few years ago, someone backed into my car. Mel and I were in the kitchen talking about how frustrated we were that we had to come up with five hundred dollars for the deductible and would have nothing to show for it. Five hundred dollars for something so useless is a lot of money! As we were talking about our frustrations, Danica left and went upstairs. She came down a few minutes later with a little baggie of coins. "Here, you can have this. Now you only need $499," she said. She has a kind and thoughtful heart. I have no doubt that Danica could subsist for the rest of her life on a steady diet of peanut butter. She almost died one year on April 1 when I skillfully installed an air horn onto our refrigerator for April Fools' Day. We're thankful she's still with us.

Kylee is a diehard gymnast and has collected an avid amount of blisters on her hands over the years from the monkey bars at school. One year when she was younger, Kylee and I ran a 5K race together. After about a mile, she looked up and said, "Dad, I can't feel my legs. Can you?" I could completely relate to how she was feeling. I smiled when she jumped as we crossed the finish line. (We waited at the finish for the other two kids, and it was a proud parent moment when each of them, without any hint or suggestion, crossed the finish line with a jump also.) It is up for debate which she loves more: her family or her sock monkey collection. She is a connoisseur of Old Maid and Mancala. She earned the Great American Award in school by completing requirements such as doing service hours, and memorizing the Gettysburg Address and all the U.S. presidents. It's not a huge surprise that she earned the award because we've bred our kids to be great Americans their whole lives by feeding them a steady diet of apple pie and bald eagles.

* * *

In my running life, I try to live without regrets. I don't want to look back and say, "I wish I had run in that location, or run a certain race. I believe that I've been blessed with a body that is willing to run (or hike, or walk, or crawl) far, and I want to take advantage of that while I can. This blessed time won't last forever.

I really strive to have the exact same approach with my family. Being a dad is a blessing, and kids grow up so quickly. My greatest fear is looking back on fatherhood and having regrets. I absolutely don't want to look back and say, "I wish I had gone out on the driveway and played more basketball with my son when he was younger." I don't want to be able to say, "I wish I had more tea parties with my daughters back when I was the coolest boy in their lives." I want to be present, involved, and dedicated as a father.

I am very conscious of the fact that being an ultrarunner demands time and focus. But I firmly believe that a hundred-mile belt buckle isn't worth sacrificing relationships with my wife or children. I try to do whatever I can to make sure that running has a minimal impact on my family life.

I vividly remember receiving a very nice compliment from my son when he was younger. Truth told, his remark wasn't meant to be a complement. We were talking about how it's important to take care of our bodies and get exercise. He said, "Well, you don't have very much room to talk. You hardly ever run."

He had no idea that I had run sixty miles that week.

I was so happy to hear his "compliment." It meant that my training for a hundred-miler hadn't taken away from family time. Ever since I started running, I have really made an effort to not let this hobby have a negative impact on my family. Time with my family is so valuable, and I want to take advantage of that.

I would love to say that I've always had a perfect balance between family and running, but I'm sure that hasn't always been the case. That balance can sometimes be a difficult tightrope to walk. Early on in my running, I felt insecure in my training, so I followed a training plan with exactness in hopes of instilling some faith in my preparedness. But this came at a cost. There were a few times when I had a long run on my training plan, so I went on the run instead of going to my son's baseball game. I felt uncomfortable with my choice, which seemed like putting running above family. I made a correction, and made sure I didn't miss anymore baseball games.

I've worked on a few tools that have helped me feel more balance between the responsibilities as a husband and father, and the desire to run long distances:

Tool #1: Be willing to sacrifice sleep. (In suggesting sacrificing sleep, I acknowledge how crucial sleep is to training, mental acuity, and recovery. For me, this balance means that I get just the amount of sleep I need ... and not much more.) I don't get quite as much sleep as I used to because almost all my running is done early in the morning or at night after kids have gone to bed. Most of the time I'm home from my run and showered before they even wake up. If it weren't for the races I do, they might not even know that I'm a runner. I'm okay with that. I'm thankful that, with a little patience, our bodies can adapt to getting a little less sleep.

Tool #2: Be willing to sacrifice television. Some non-runners may consider this ridiculous and inconceivable. But there are only so many hours in a day. If running is a priority, those hours need to come from somewhere. Aside from a few minutes of the news each night, I don't watch much TV. Sometimes I'll be running late at night and pass houses where I can see someone sitting on their couch watching TV. I think to myself, "What is this crazy hobby I'm involved in? I could be sitting on my couch watching "Seinfeld" with some Ben & Jerry's in my hand ... but instead I'm out in the dark sweating my guts out and getting eaten by mosquitoes!"

I fully admit feelings of jealousy when I hear friends or coworkers talking about their favorite season of "Breaking Bad," while I haven't seen even one episode. I have twinges of envy when I hear people talking about their weekend binge watching Netflix. That sounds really fun!

I was actually having these same thoughts while I ran alone on a trail around sunset one night. I was dumping sweat by the gallon and being eaten alive by mosquitoes. I thought, "You know, maybe I'm missing out. Maybe I need to relax and do what so many other people are doing. It sounds enjoyable to just crash in front of the TV and vegetate."

Then a few minutes later the sun was setting, barely hovering above the horizon. At that moment, the red cliffs on the horizon began to glow in the sunset. The sky turned bright yellow and orange and pink. And despite the fact that the summer night was sweltering hot, I got goosebumps. I thought, "Okay. What I'm witnessing right now far surpasses anything I could be watching on TV." I felt so thankful for the amazing beauty that was encompassing me. My views put "Breaking Bad" to shame.

One of my ultrarunning heroes is my friend Carol Manwaring. One day when I was picking her brain about ultramarathons, she said something that has stuck with me: "I think almost anyone could do this if they spent less time on the couch in front of the TV." If you're struggling with finding time to exercise, look into how many hours a week you spend in front of the TV or on social media.

Tool #3: Compromise. Mel and I often trade time. She'll say, "You go out and run for a few hours, then tonight I'll go out to dinner and a movie with my sisters while you watch the kids." Sometimes I'll make deals with the kids. "I'm going to run ten miles. Then, when I get home, if the house isn't burned down and your mom isn't bald from pulling all her hair out, we'll go get ice cream." They've never been the type to turn down ice cream.

Tool #4: Make running a family activity. There are a few ways I have made this work for me. Sometimes we'll go to the track as a family. Whoever wants to run can run. Whoever wants to play Frisbee on the field can play Frisbee. But we're there together, and spending time with each other while getting some activity. Another way my family enjoys being involved in running is by coming to races. They make signs, come and cheer at aid stations, and during some hundred-milers, they'll join me when I cross the finish line.

Tool #5: Spend quality time together that has nothing to do with running. One night, we got ambitious and had our first ever family campout in the living room. I pulled the girls' mattresses into the living room for me and Mel to sleep on, and then the kids set up little beds around us. We just hung out and watched episodes of "I Love Lucy" and "America's Funniest Videos." We ate brownies and ice cream. We laughed together. As we were laying there going to sleep, I couldn't help thinking that this was pure happiness to be spending time with my wife and kids like this.

I try to really strive for the idea that if running does cut into time with family a little bit, it becomes that much more important for the time that we do spend together to be quality time. In my actions I try to show that although running is important to me, it is by no means the most important thing to me. I want my family to see that they are my priority. No belt buckle, no PR, no finish line, no toned body, no accomplishment is worth sacrificing the relationships that matter most to me. Words are inadequate to express my gratitude for Mel, Jackson, Danica, and Kylee. They are my rock of encouragement.

13) It's Fun and Impresses The Opposite Sex

Running with buffaloes on Antelope Island

Y ou know you are in for an adventure when registration for the race requires signing the following waiver:

"I know that there are hazards associated with running this race. These hazards can include, but are not limited to, bikers, hikers, horses, very large wild animals, roots, rocks, trees, other assorted wildlife, flora and fauna, and other crazed runners. I also agree that by running the ultra, I know I'm nuts and should know better than to do something like this, but, hey, it's fun and impresses the opposite sex."

The Antelope Island Buffalo Run is an ultramarathon held on Antelope Island in the middle of the Great Salt Lake. The race derives its name from the fact that there are hundreds of buffalo on the island. I fully admit that I felt more than a little apprehensive when I read on the website that "bison will charge you (and not with credit cards) if you enter their personal space. The charges are generally short but can result in having to clean out your shorts, and that leads to chafing issues. Don't look them directly in the eye; they take it as a challenge."

Running the race seemed like a death wish. The first distance I signed up to run there was the fifty-miler. I was beginning to think that if running fifty miles didn't kill me, a grumpy herd of bison would. Fortunately I finished the race without any "clean out your shorts" experiences. I knew I was running with right group of people during the race when I heard one guy say to the other, "The cutoff for the race is twelve hours and thirty minutes. If you finish any faster than twelve hours and thirty minutes, you aren't getting your money's worth."

At one aid station I came across Jay Aldous, who at the time held the World Record for the fastest hundred-miler for someone age fifty to fifty-four. He was volunteering at the race and was full of enthusiasm and encouragement. "How are you feeling Cory? How can I help you?"

I drank a cup of Coke and he made sure I had everything I needed before I left. Then he said, "Do you want one more cup of Coke before you leave just in case? You can always throw it up later." That is certainly difficult reasoning to argue with. So I drank another cup of Coke.

I had such a positive experience running the fifty-miler that I signed up to run a hundred miles at the Buffalo Run the following year. In the week leading up to the race, I nervously watched the weather forecast.

Seven days before the race, there was snow in the forecast. This was great news because the actual weather is usually the complete opposite of what the forecast predicts a week beforehand. But with each passing day, a pounding of snow was predicted to hit Antelope Island.

The forecast stayed the same up to the day before the race, so I packed plenty of warm clothes. It's a good thing, because we got our first taste of snow within the first hour of the race. There was a wind so frigid and stinging that it felt as though it was blowing through every layer of clothing I wore.

When I run races, I enjoy talking with other runners along the way. I talked with two runners who told me they were a father/son duo. I said, "Wow, that is so awesome!" But then the dad said that his eighty-one-year-old father, Grant, was also running the hundred-miler! This completely blew my mind.

"I would love to meet him!" I said. He assured me that I would. He told me that Grant had been approved for an early start, so he was somewhere up ahead of us on the trail.

"Dad has a bad back so he leans over to the side. When you see a guy up ahead that is shaped like an upside down L, you'll know you've found him."

Sure enough, after a few miles I saw a runner up ahead who was leaning to the side. When I caught up with him, I said, "Hi Grant! Your son and grandson told me all about you. I think you are such an inspiration." I talked with him for a bit, took a picture, and then continued on down the trail.

The extreme winter weather forced Grant to stop after fifty miles, which is nothing short of spectacular. How completely amazing is it that an eighty-one-year-old man would have the bravery to click "Register" for a hundred-mile race? It goes to show that age doesn't need to be a limiting factor in going after your dreams.

This race has a noon start time, so by the time I reached mile thirty, it was getting dark. I was starting to feel tired, and I was in no-man's land for a while. There wasn't another runner ahead of or behind me for as far as I could see. I started to hit a rough patch where I wasn't feeling good, so when I arrived at an aid station, I decided to sit for a few minutes to regroup and eat a quesadilla and some bacon. Because when does bacon not make things better?

As I was sitting in the aid station tent, the front flap of the tent opened and another runner walked in. It was Marty Harward, who I had met for the first time earlier in the race. We had run much of the first fifteen miles together, and now here he was again. We decided to stick together and help each other get to mile fifty, where we would each have pacers waiting. It was a relief to have the company of another runner through the night, and I was again reminded of the deep bonds of friendship that can be built on the trails. Someone is helping you through a difficult time, and you're doing the same thing for them in return.

I look back on a photo that was taken of me and Marty after we reached the fifty-mile aid station at 12:45 a.m. Our faces were red from many hours in the bitter cold air. My eyes were bloodshot. Marty's eyes were squinting from the onslaught of winter wind blowing at us. And our smiles were enormous.

Can I tell you a little secret about that happy, smiling picture of me and Marty? We were miserable. Absolutely, positively miserable. Tired. Sore. Frozen solid. But what I find so inspiring at these ultramarathons is the mentality of the runners. Despite the adversity and exhaustion, almost everyone is amazingly positive. I would see runners truly suffering and ask how they were doing. Their response was almost always "Good!" or "Great!" They didn't focus on everything going wrong, only on what was going right. And sometimes the only thing going right was that we were still upright.

At mile fifty, I picked up my first pacer — my sister Hollie. The next eighteen miles with her were incredibly challenging. I heard that with the bitter wind blowing across the island, the wind chill was eight degrees. Hollie did a miraculous job of plowing ahead of me, and I worked to keep up with her over some more technical, hilly trails. I can't imagine doing that by myself. My wife has told me that my race reports sometimes minimize the dark spots. And not the "dark" of night. The kind of mental darkness where you think about quitting. The darkness where you don't know how you can keep going. The incredible discouragement when you realize that you are beyond exhausted and still have fifty (*fifty*!) more miles to go. I definitely had some of those dark moments. Those moments are hard to describe in words. It's like someone is holding a blanket over you, smothering and suffocating. I tried to have faith that if I could make it through the night, I would get new life with the sunrise.

I picked up my second pacer, Jared Thorley, at mile sixty-eight. He planned to join me for the rest of the race. In an apologetic tone I said, "I'm sorry, Jared. My legs are just shot. I don't think I'll be able to run a single step for the last thirty miles of the race." Jared and I are very much alike. He knew that being a demanding, drill sergeant-like pacer wasn't what I needed. He was patient and understanding when he smiled and said, "That's fine. We'll just do the best we can do."

I told Jared to go up ahead of me, keep a steady pace, and I'd do my best to keep up with him. Somewhere around this time I had a breakthrough. My knees were crazy sore and my feet felt like I was walking on hot coals. Every step hurt. But I realized that it only hurt a little more to run. So I wondered, "Why not just run and get this over with?"

I would mutter to Jared, "Okay, let's run for a bit." I'd go as long as my legs could bear and then cry Uncle, and he would go back to a fast power walk. We kept doing that as the miles ticked by. Around mile ninety, my suffering was still at a tolerable level. I told Jared that if we kept up this pace, I could beat my previous hundred-mile PR (personal record) of twenty-nine hours and twenty-two minutes. I told him how cool it would be to see a PR that started with twenty-eight. Jared said, "If you stick with me, I can get you a PR that starts with twenty-seven!" That lit a fire in me. I really wanted that. I wasn't sure it was possible, but I was willing to try. I tried to turn off all the complaining in my brain and just run like a mad man.

During the last ten miles, I was running harder than I ever had at the end of a race. I then had what I can only describe as a crazy out-of-body experience. I had never felt that way before, and haven't felt that way since. I felt like someone slipped some acid into my Mountain Dew. (No mom, I haven't really used acid.) I could hear myself talking and I could see my legs moving below me, but it didn't feel like me.

As I was running along the trail, it felt like I floated outside my body. I just floated a foot above myself, watching this nerdy, gangly runner head down the trail. I knew that feet were running below me, but I couldn't feel them. I heard myself saying things to Jared, but it sounded like someone far away yelling through a tunnel. It was beyond strange. I didn't like it.

I heard myself say, "I feel really weird. I think I'm going to pass out."

Jared's response was exactly what I needed to hear. "You're not going to pass out," he said which a chuckle. "Just keep running."

Jared was right. I didn't pass out. And I did, indeed, keep running. All the while thinking, "I just want to sit down and watch Judge Judy while inhaling large quantities of chocolate chip cookies."

I crossed the finish line and looked down at my watch in disbelief. Twenty-seven hours and forty-four minutes. A PR that started with twenty-seven.

* * *

In 2014, I was invited back to the race to accompany my friends Clair Coleman and Catherine Kalian on Antelope Island. They were going for their first hundred-mile finishes. Not only were they my coworkers, but they were also two of my best friends. Catherine is like the sister you always wished you had: constantly happy, occasionally belittling but only when deserved, and incessantly funny. Clair is like a father figure. An athletic, humble, hilarious father figure. I couldn't resist the opportunity to join them on a hundred-mile adventure at the Antelope Island Buffalo Run. We planned to run every single one of those hundred miles together.

Hundred-mile races are like a box of chocolates. You never know what you're going to get. (What can I say, I'm a sucker for Forrest Gump's cross-country run.) Maybe during the race you'll open up that symbolic box of chocolate and get some awesome friends to run with. Maybe you'll roll your ankle so bad that it will bring you to tears. Maybe you'll get to an aid station serving cinnamon rolls that taste just like they were handmade by Jesus himself. Maybe you'll have an unforgettable, incredible hundred miles. During that race, I experienced all of those things.

Catherine and I saw a funny dance video the week before the race, and I thought it was high time that someone made an ultramarathon dance video. I figured it could be seriously awesome. She concurred. During the race, we ran to this beautiful overlook, I switched on the camera, and she did a little dance. Then everything changed. In a crazy fluke of chance, Catherine landed wrong on her ankle. She twisted it in a direction that an ankle should never twist, touching her ankle to the ground, which should never happen. She immediately crumpled into a heap on the dirt. This was at mile eight. *Eight.* Thankfully my friend Eric, who happens to be a physician assistant, was there when it happened. He felt around the area and said it would get swollen but with the degree of the sprain, it wouldn't cause damage if she kept going.

I think most people would have dropped from the race. Catherine did not. (Disclaimer: I'm not advocating running through an injury or doing something that would cause damage. Don't do something dumb just to be cool. She actually checked with a number of other medical personnel as well.) We continued down the trail.

One of the greatest parts for me during the race was having Mel and Jackson helping out as crew at various aid stations. After the race, I thanked them for all their help. Jackson said, "Well, I didn't really do much." I told him that he had no idea how encouraging and energizing it is just to see a familiar face. I was so grateful for their support.

We got to the fifty-mile mark in the middle of the night. It was dreadfully cold and windy. We each picked up a pacer. Mine was my friend Danny Widerberg, who kept us entertained with stories of racing, and how running helped transform his broken life and family into the beautiful life he has now. He said when he tucks his little boys in at night, he will occasionally say, "I love one of you so much," as he closes their door ... then listens to them argue about which one is loved. Or if the kids act up, he'll say, "When your real dad gets out of prison, I'm sending you right back to him." He helped get us through a solid twenty miles during the middle of the night.

My friend and pacer extraordinaire, Jared Thorley, who helped get me to the finish line the year before, joined us to pace for the last thirty miles. It's nice to have a fresh face to distract you from the bone-chilling wind and the sensation that someone is doing the Riverdance on your legs. Around mile eighty-five, I reached that inevitable point in a hundred-miler when you are beyond exhaustion. Your feet are not happy campers. You would sell your soul for a shower and a bed. And you absolutely cannot begin to wrap your head around how you are going to go another fifteen miles. That is an unbelievably daunting part of the race. The only thing you can do is be determined enough to keep putting one foot in front of the other. At that precise moment of concern and fear, we arrived at an aid station that had cinnamon rolls. They tasted like icing-coated morsels of heaven and provided instant happiness.

Our caravan of runners and pacers proceeded down the trail. Every once in a while we'd stop to stretch, laugh a little, and try to not collapse. Jared serenaded us with an ear-piercing rendition of "Kokomo" by the Beach Boys, but I was too weak by this time to pop him in the mouth. Words can't adequately describe that feeling of happiness when after just a hair over twenty-nine hours of running, you see that goal that has taken blood, sweat, and tears to achieve: the finish line. We grabbed hands as we crossed the line, and I told Catherine and Clair, "You will never be the same from this moment on."

It was quite a remarkable experience to spend an entire hundred miles with the same people. That rarely happens in a race. People go through their high points and low points at different times, so it takes a willingness to see each other through their hard times. It was rewarding to be able to help them through the periods where they were struggling, and to have them do the exact same thing for me.

14) Resisting The Urge To Hug Random Mountain Bikers

Getting myself into a risky situation on Gooseberry Mesa

One common question people ask when they learn that I run trails is, "Do you ever get scared being out in the wilderness alone?" The answer is a resounding "no." I have had more dangerous close calls running on roads. I couldn't count how many times I've been running on the road and watched a car pass by while the driver is staring at a phone, completely oblivious to the fact that they just sped past a runner only a few feet away. For me, being out in the wilderness alone is exactly what I love about trail running.

There have only been two times when I felt a bit nervous out on the trails. The first was when I came around a curve on a trail covered with tumbleweeds and nearly stepped on a rattlesnake. The second was during a run while I was training for the first Zion 100, which was being held in May. The month of May in southern Utah can be scorching hot, so I made an effort to get adequate heat training.

I planned to do a twenty-one-mile run to the top of Gooseberry Mesa. I added a few extra layers of clothing just to make sure I was plenty warm. As I was packing for the run, I noticed a small hole in the bladder of my hydration pack. So instead of hassling with trying to patch it, I threw two bottles of water into the pack and took two more handheld bottles.

The route I took to the top of Gooseberry Mesa is a mile and a half of trail that is nearly vertical. I have never been on a trail longer and steeper than the climb to the top of Gooseberry. I made it to the top, and then explored the punishing slickrock trails at the top of the mesa. After eleven miles, I decided to turn around and head back the way I came. I stopped to check how much water I had left in my pack and immediately got a sick, sinking feeling in my stomach. I had eleven miles to get back to the car and I was starting to run low on water.

I realized I had made a mistake. I had worn too many layers. It was too hot outside. And I didn't bring enough water. Though I was in trouble, I knew it wasn't yet an emergency. Gooseberry Mesa is a hotspot for mountain bikers. It was a weekday afternoon so bike traffic would be significantly less, but I hoped that if I got desperate I'd see at least one mountain biker.

I hate asking others for help, but after a few miles my panic slowly increased. I saw a mountain biker coming toward me and I swallowed my pride. As he passed I said, "Hey, do you have a little bit of water to spare?" The fact that I was willing to even ask was an indication of how much I was in need. My panic increased even more when he said, "I'm sorry, I don't."

An hour later I was out of water and was overheating. A wave of relief washed over me when I saw three mountain bikers coming up but my pride got the best of me. I felt so utterly foolish for letting myself get into this situation that I couldn't bring myself to ask for help. I stood on the trail silently as they passed.

After they passed, I heard them stop for a minute to enjoy the view before them. I turned around and went back to them. I said, "Do you guys happen to have a little bit of extra water?" I told them I still had an hour or two to go and I was out of water. In an instant all three of them had their packs off offering to fill my bottles. They were truly an answer to prayers. I'm convinced they were angels with bike helmets and sweat-stained jerseys. I could have hugged them.

Another forty-five minutes later I saw a camper up ahead. My water was almost out again, and I still had a brutally steep descent off the mesa followed by a few more miles. I prayed that someone would be in the camper to spare some water. I knocked on the door and called out but nobody answered. I got that sick feeling in my stomach again. Then I saw a table sitting at the front of the camper with a box of bottled water on top. Another prayer answered. I figured they wouldn't mind sparing a bottle and I used it to get me back to my car.

In the hundreds and hundreds of miles I have run alone on trails, this was the only time I have ever felt like I put myself in a bad situation. I am normally overly prepared and it is important for me to be safe, so this was uncharacteristic. I felt so incredibly grateful for the kindness of strangers and resolved that I would pay it forward. In the wise words of Susan Donnelly, it was an "unnecessary amount of epic-ness per mile." That mistake taught me that in trail running, it's not enough to be prepared, or even overly prepared. Extreme care should be taken in preparation, even for the most routine training runs.

15) I Was One Of Those Zombies

Experiences at the Zion 100

t was taking everything I had to not throw up. I felt like I was standing in a toaster oven set to high and could almost hear my skin sizzling. My vision was a little fuzzy and I prayed I wouldn't pass out. I swear I saw vultures circling over me. And then crossed the finish line of the Zion 100.

Now rewind to thirty-five hours and a hundred miles earlier. I found myself standing at the starting line with 117 fellow runners ready to take on a challenge so daunting that I couldn't let my mind get caught on the details or else I might start crying: run one hundred miles in fewer than thirty-six hours through the desert, up and down enormous mesas, in the middle of ninety-plus-degree heat, and, if at all possible, avoid dying. Although there was certainly a part of me that was scared, there was also a huge part of me that was beyond excited.

The course of the Zion 100 was drastically different from my first hundred miler at Javelina Jundred. These trails on the outskirts of Zion National Park in southern Utah weren't the rolling hills of Arizona. It wasn't like comparing apples to oranges. It was like comparing apples to ostriches.

Despite the significantly more challenging course, I did have one thing in my favor: home field advantage. Living in Hurricane, Utah, I can hit most of the Zion 100 course within a twenty minute drive from my house. I can roll out of bed and get a quick run on the rolling singletrack of the JEM Trail before work. A quick drive up the Dalton Wash dirt road will put me on the twisting slick rock of the Guacamole Trail. I can see the towering red majesty of Gooseberry Mesa from my driveway. I considered it an enormous advantage to be familiar with a majority of the course before the race even started.

The Zion 100 didn't waste much time giving us runners a swift slap across the face. Only a few miles into the race, we were met with our first of many challenges for the day: climbing the Flying Monkey Trail to get to the top of Smith Mesa. The history of the mesa wasn't lost on me as I climbed a thousand feet into the sky within the span of one mile.

In the 1950s, jet propulsion in military aircraft was all the rage. But with higher aircraft speed came the need for improvements in ejection seats for pilots. In 1953, the Air Force awarded a $2 million contract for the construction of the Supersonic Military Air Research Track to test ejection seats.

A track twelve thousand feet long was constructed atop the mesa, which ended at the edge of the cliff, plunging into the valley below. At the time, it was the longest rocket research track in the United States. At first, test dummies were launched off the mesa at 1,050 miles per hour to test ejection seats. But reportedly, those test dummies were later replaced with chimpanzees; hence the name: the Flying Monkey Trail. Our very first climb of the race was high enough to launch rockets. Race director Matt Gunn is known for going the extra mile to put on exemplary races, and even had someone dressed in a full-body monkey costume to greet runners as we arrived at the top of the mesa.

I planned to run most of the race by myself. I train alone and love the solitude. But within the first mile I seemed to be keeping the exact same pace with a few other guys. I couldn't have imagined at the time that I would end up covering more than sixty miles with them. In those many, many hours I built close friendships with Ben, Travis, and Eric.

It was around noon and the temperature continued to climb. We could see that runners were starting to suffer. We came across one guy curled up under a little bush. He was trying to find some shade and was almost out of water. We shared some of ours, but this was still early in the race, and I realized how much of an impact the heat would have. Even though I was really hot, I was thankful I hadn't reached the point of curling up under a bush. After the guy assured us that he'd be okay, we pushed on.

This was the first hundred-miler for Ben and Travis, but Eric was the wise master of the group. This was Eric's thirtieth hundred-miler, not to mention a handful of 350-milers. I think each of us was a little bit like a middle school girl around Justin Bieber with Eric. He kept us laughing the whole time and was full of insights and tips. Around mile thirty, Eric found an old tennis ball on the side of the road with a slit in it. We all laughed at him throwing it around, almost oblivious to the fact that he was in the middle of a grueling hundred-mile ultramarathon. When he squeezed the ball, the slit would open up and it looked like a smiling mouth.

Travis said, "I wish we had a Sharpie marker so we could draw a face on it!" I am not lying — less than two miles later we were cruising down the trail and guess what Ben saw sitting on the dirt? A SHARPIE MARKER! When was the last time you found a marker on your trail run? Never? Me neither. This was a good omen. Our wish was granted. That tennis ball now had a face.

We all rolled into mile thirty-five together. This was my first opportunity to see my family. They were so happy and encouraging, and this gave me a huge emotional boost. Jackson said, "Dad, your eyes are really red. You have dark rings under your eyes. You look like you would pay lots of money to take a nap for one hour." His comment was very perceptive. And very accurate.

At mile thirty-five, a switch flipped for my entire race. At that moment, I entered a time warp. My legs were moving and it appeared that I was running, but it felt like I was going nowhere. We would run and hike for hours, and it felt like landmarks up ahead weren't getting any closer. Miles thirty-five to forty-two were agonizingly long. It was the hottest part of the day and temps said ninety-two degrees, but out on the desert floor the heat radiated up at us and it felt much hotter. We were truly running inside an Easy Bake Oven, although it was certainly a beautiful Easy Bake Oven.

My stomach had gone into outright rebellion by this point. The possibility of throwing up seemed inevitable. I desperately didn't want to get regurgitated Gatorade on my shoes. The aid station at mile forty-two was not a pretty sight. One lady looked like she was barfing up a lung. People were laying down trying to cool off and get their stomachs back.

Right after this aid station we started the hardest section of the entire race — climbing to the top of Gooseberry Mesa. Ascending more than 1,500 feet in less than a mile, the route up to Gooseberry is as close to vertical as you'll find in a race. We didn't talk much during the climb. Mainly because it's difficult to talk when your lungs are filling with molten lava. Travis was feeling so bad that he turned around halfway up the mesa. He walked back to the aid station and dropped out of the race.

The miles on top of Gooseberry are technical and very difficult in the daylight, but indescribably more challenging in the dark. The rolling, twisting slickrock all looks the same in the dark, and it is easy to get turned around without even knowing it. Many runners got lost, some going in circles without realizing what was happening.

I was so incredibly thankful to do those eighteen miles on Gooseberry in the dark with Ben and Eric. Sometimes we got off track and it took all three of us to find our way back to the trail. We met other runners who were alone and got off track and we got them going the right direction. Around mile sixty-five, I was out of juice. My body was spent, and I couldn't keep pace with Eric and Ben anymore. I thanked them for their companionship and helping me get through many difficult miles, then told them to leave me because they were in much better condition at the moment than I was.

I picked up my first pacer at mile seventy. Jess Jensen has been a friend of mine for many years, and I was honored that she wanted to spend miles seventy through ninety with me. Jess is always positive, encouraging, and funny. I was so grateful to have her with me. Exhaustion had fully kicked in and I was feeling weary. At mile eighty-two, the sun was up again. It was so discouraging to come to the realization that I would have another full day of heat. My family came out to meet me at the mile eighty-two aid station, but even a visit from them couldn't shake the fear I had of the next eighteen miles.

The many hours with Jess were gut-wrenchingly slow. My nausea kept coming and going, my rear end felt like it was getting kicked by a donkey with every single step, and my feet … oh, sweet mercy, my feet.

At mile ninety, I met up with Mel to pace me the last ten miles. We were right back to ninety-plus-degree temperatures. I was getting a little foggy and hoped that I wouldn't pass out because that would be rather embarrassing. In those fuzzy hours I thought about how complex it is to run a hundred miles. During a marathon, you eat a gel every once in a while, get some water every other mile, and keep going until you're done in three to six hours. During a hundred-miler you have to:

1) Monitor your pace so you have enough energy to get you to the finish.

2) Be diligent about eating around two-hundred to three-hundred calories per hour.

3) Closely monitor hydration. Too little water can cause very big problems. Too much water can cause very big problems. Hydration has to be exact.

4) Monitor bodily functioning. Peeing too much? Too little? Too light? Too dark? (Sorry, too much information?)

5) Take varying amounts of salt or electrolytes depending on temperature, sweat, and exertion level.

6) Closely scan the trail ahead and know where every rock is so you don't fall or sprain an ankle.

7) Pay attention to your feet and handle hot spots/blisters immediately.

8) Figure out how to handle your stomach if (or when) you want to barf your guts out.

9) Figure out how to deal with exhaustion when you feel like you can't take one more step but you still have twenty miles to go.

10) Try to ignore your brain when it is begging you stop and yelling excuses for why it's okay to quit. But here's the kicker: YOU HAVE TO DO EACH OF THESE THINGS SIMULTANEOUSLY. If you screw up any of these, you may not see the finish line. And even if you do them all perfectly, something else may come up. This constant monitoring is extremely exhausting both physically and mentally. Thankfully, Mel was there to keep me on track. There was nobody I'd rather spend those last ten miles with.

With what little emotion and energy I had left, I was so thankful and excited to make it to the finish line. After thirty-four hours, fifty-nine minutes, and fifty-nine seconds (we'll just say thirty-five hours), I jumped across the finish line of the Zion 100. (And then I jumped across it a few more times because the family wanted to get a good picture.)

* * *

When I ran the race again in 2013, I arrived at the Guacamole Trail aid station in the middle of the night. Steve and Kendra Hooper and Turd'l Miller from St. George Running Center were manning the aid station. I bought my very first pair of running shoes from the St. George Running Center and have been friends with these people ever since. I walked up to the aid station table and Turd'l said with an enormous smile, "Hey Cory! It's awesome to see you! What can I get you? What sounds good? Do you want a cinnamon apple pancake?"

I thought for a second, then responded, "Yeah, actually that sounds pretty good."

I ate the pancake and it was absolutely amazing! It was gone in three seconds flat. Then he said, "How about a raspberry pancake?"

My response: "Definitely! Wow, you guys have quite the food selection up here!" I inhaled another pancake.

Then a girl walked up and whispered, "You know that he's just pouring Hammer Gel on the pancake, right?"

At mile 83, I reached Whiskeytown, the aid station at the home of my friends George and Melissa Walsh. When I saw them earlier, at mile ten, they said that they had a cinnamon roll waiting at their house. I thought they were kidding. Yet, when I got to mile eighty-three, I realized they weren't kidding. I arrived and they handed me a cinnamon roll the size of my face. Their kindness really touched me. (And that sugar rush got me through another mile or two.) This was the first time someone giving me a cinnamon roll ever got me choked up.

* * *

I ran Zion again in 2014, when Turd'l, who had essentially become the Julia Child of ultramarathon aid stations, had a new concoction for me to try: tortillas smeared with Nutella, followed by a sugar cookie in the middle. Genius! Pure genius! My only regret was that Turd'l couldn't be at every single aid station.

And then, to keep my Zion 100 streak going, I ran the 2015 race also. I saw zombies stumbling all over the place. A dim lightbulb of realization flickered when I realized that I *was* one of those zombies! It was in the middle of the Utah desert. The heat was somewhere around 8,172 degrees. I've never seen the show "The Walking Dead," but I'm convinced that they could film the show at mile ninety of hundred-milers and avoid paying lots of money for a cast.

At least the zombies were friendly. They just wanted to get to the finish line, have someone hand them a belt buckle, take off their shoes, and try to avoid dry heaving. This is the awesomeness of an ultramarathon.

Again we were given an abrupt welcome from the Flying Monkey Trail. One section is so steep that there is a strategically placed rope to hoist up your not-dead-yet body. As I seem to have a problem with at every race, I took a casket load of pictures (um, around three hundred during this particular race.)

As though going UP Flying Monkey wasn't fun enough, we also had the pleasure of going back DOWN Flying Monkey due to some new course changes. Going down can be as tricky as going up when your legs have become floppy and the angle of the trail is so steep that one misstep catching your toe on a rock could cause you to summersault down in a bloody cloud of dust.

At the Zion 100, what goes down must go up. And then down. And then up. And then back down again. You get the point. So after getting back down the Flying Monkey Trail, we climbed back up a different section of the course to reach the Guacamole Trail. The undulating, relentless slickrock makes your calves feel like they are being rubbed by cheese graters.

After lots of cheese grater miles, we went back down the same way we came, and then headed toward the trail torture chamber that is the climb to the top of Gooseberry Mesa. On my way there, I had my scariest experience ever while running. I was running with my friend Terri Rashid. We were nearing a wide valley on the desert floor when we were suddenly enveloped in a cloud of bees. I have never seen anything like it. They were all around us. Here's the thing — I'm deathly allergic to bees. I carry an Epi-Pen in my pack to quickly inject myself with epinephrine in hopes of preventing an allergic reaction if I did happen to get stung by a bee, but even then, a bee sting would at best end my race for the day, and at worst, leave me in serious trouble. I stood still as the swarm of bees surrounded us. I have never felt more terrified and helpless. But a few seconds later, the bees left and neither of us received a solitary sting. It was truly a miracle. Yet again I had the conviction that guardian angels were watching over me.

I finally arrived at the beast named Gooseberry. It's loose dirt and rock, so it feels like turning an ice skating rink at a forty-five degree angle and then trying to climb up it. (And then of course there is the challenge of going back DOWN this trail at mile sixty-nine … in the dark … when your legs feel like chocolate pudding.)

When Meatloaf sang, "I would do anything for love, but I won't do that," he was singing about climbing up the Gooseberry Trail. Even the most manly man in the world, Chuck Norris, would have a sobbing, emotional breakdown if he saw this trail. If you are able to disconnect from your own suffering for a moment, it is hilarious to watch everyone go up this thing. They take three steps, then hunch over to catch their breath. Three steps, hunch over to catch their breath. Three steps, hunch over to catch their breath. This scene is remarkably less hilarious when you're the one doing the hunching.

I took one jumping picture during the race. It was at mile forty-one at a location called The Point, on the very edge of the mesa. It is my favorite part of the whole course. If you're going to take one jumping picture during a race, this is undoubtedly the spot to take it.

Much to my horror, I had a tragic wardrobe malfunction. I set my camera on the ground, started the ten-second self-timer, and then jumped in the air right at the time of exposure. But the camera wasn't the only thing doing an exposure. As I was up in the air, I kicked my legs apart and felt my shorts rip right at the crotch region. Was the jumping picture worth the wardrobe malfunction? Indeed! And I was incredibly thankful for the spare pair of shorts I had stashed in a drop bag at the next aid station.

I tried a new foot lube (yes, breaking a cardinal rule of running which is to never trying something new on race day). It worked well and prevented my feet from getting blisters, but it made one of my shoes squeak. Each time the shoe hit the ground, it sounded like a cat meowing. I know it wasn't the shoes because I wore the exact same pair of Altra Olympus shoes at Monument Valley the month prior and didn't have any issues. If you think running an ultra would drive you crazy, try having a cat meow at you every other step for a hundred miles!

I was once again blessed to have Mel and Jackson crew almost the whole time. They met me at aid stations, helped get supplies, provided moral support, and at one stop even had chips and queso dip in the car. (Lacking every ounce of self-control by that point, I proceeded to eat WAY more chips and queso than a human being should be eating in the midst of a hundred-miler.) Having this family support meant so much to me. At sunset I saw them one last time before they headed home for the night.

After they left, I headed out into the darkness of night. I was at one of those low points where I felt really tired and zapped of energy. I didn't think about dropping out but wondered how in the world I could keep going for another fifty miles. (The answer to that question: one step at a time.)

In the middle of the night, I struggled mightily to stay awake. I loathe that feeling of sleep-walking and then stumbling myself awake. I decided I'd lay down right in the middle of the trail and take a shoe nap … I mean cat nap. (Get it?) I figured laying in the middle of the trail would assure that I wouldn't sleep too long. I kept my headlamp on, thinking that might prevent a mountain lion from eating me. I glanced at my watch then tried to sleep. I made it precisely two minutes before runners arrived and asked if I was okay. Cat nap attempt over. Time to keep moving. After approximately eternity, I saw my second sunrise of the race.

With the rising sun, I started seeing mountain bikers on the trails. I wanted to body slam them into the slickrock and then steal their bike so I could ride the remaining miles instead of running them. Then I remembered that the muscle composition of my body is .04 percent, so I just let them pass instead. Mel and Jackson came out to crew again on the second day, and Mel ran with me for seven miles at the end of the race. She kept me moving well and ignored those times when an involuntary whimper would escape my mouth.

I was so happy to be done after thirty-two hours and change that I knelt down kissed the ground beneath my feet. It won't come as much of a surprise that I found getting down was significantly easier than getting up. At the Zion 100, each buckle is handmade and unique using materials from the course. I looked at lots of buckles and finally found one that whispered that it wanted to come home with me.

Ultramarathons have a way of stripping you bare. All the outside layers are peeled away like an onion and you are left alone with your doubts and fears and a finish line that feels like an eternity away. But step after step, minute after minute, hour after hour that finish line gets closer. And when you find it all the doubts and fears vanish, replaced by triumph.

16) Mosquitoes Sucked Out My Dignity

Unusual experiences during ultramarathon training

As much as I love races, I also love the training that goes into preparing for a race. A hefty supply of training miles lends itself to having an ample supply of crazy experiences during those training miles.

One night after work, I headed out for a thirty-mile training run. It had been a busy week, and the only time I had to get a long run in was on Friday night after work. My route took me on a big loop around Hurricane, Utah. I circled Sand Hollow Reservoir without a glimpse of civilization, alone in the dark for many miles. Finally after a few hours of running, I reached humanity again and may have (did) stop at a gas station to fill my water bottle with Coke.

At mile twenty-three, I was starving. It was almost midnight and I hadn't eaten since noon. I knew there was a Wendy's ahead, and hoped that they would still be open. Thankfully the drive-through was! I sheepishly walked up to the drive-through. But they said their rules required that you couldn't *walk* through a *drive*-through. They refused to serve any food. I almost started crying.

Literally ten seconds later an angel appeared. A car pulled up to the drive-through. I planned to ask the random stranger if I could give him some money and have him order food for me. As the driver rolled down the window to place his order I saw that it was one of my dialysis patients! I hoped I wasn't hallucinating.

I said, "Wow! I'm so happy to see you! If I gave you some money, would you buy a few hamburgers for me?" Of course he did. Those two bacon cheeseburgers and fries were the best food I ate all week. Granted, I had gut rot and chunky burps for the next hour (shocker) but it was more than worth it.

It was during a different thirty-mile training run that I had the most embarrassing moment of my life (right behind that time when I was nine years old, shopping for school clothes, and a lady opened the door of my dressing room while I was standing there in my tighty whities).

I had run eight miles when I passed through some long stretches of farm fields. From past experience, I knew the mosquitoes were horrible here, but I didn't put bug spray on before the run because it was raining. (I put a poncho in my pack just in case it started to downpour.)

Unfortunately, by the time I reached the fields, it had stopped raining. I started to feel a few mosquitoes on my legs.

I ran faster. "Maybe if I'm moving faster they won't be able to catch me," I thought. But they did catch me. Sweet mercy did they ever catch me. I don't know why, but mosquitoes think I am the most attractive human ever created. My wife and I can go running and she'll get home with a mosquito bite. I'll have fifty. Literally. And they swell up to the size of Junior Mints.

So I realize that they are swarming all over my legs. I'm running like the dickens. Then a horrific thing happened: I looked behind me. I was surrounded by a cloud of mosquitoes. My neck and arms and back were covered. They were sucking my blood through my shirt.

I ran faster. I had this vision in my mind of someone coming across my bones on the side of the road. And a coroner doing an autopsy and then telling my family that I had succumbed to Death By Mosquito.

"Run, Cory! RUN!" said a voice in my brain.

By this point I was experiencing my first-ever panic attack. I didn't want to stop and pull out my phone to call my wife because I knew if I stopped for even a split second I would get an extra hundred bites. And then I took off my head phones and that's when the panic attack reached epic proportions. It sounded like a swarm of angry hornets.

"AAAAAHHHHHH!" said that voice in my brain.

That was the tipping point. I stopped and got the phone out of my pack and called my wife. Our conversation went like this:

Me: "Help! I'm being attacked my mosquitoes over by the farms!"

Mel: "Okay, I'm on my way."

Me: "Please! Hurry!"

Mel: "Do you have your poncho?"

Me: "Yes, but that won't help at all! It doesn't cover my legs!"

Mel: "Sit down on the ground and put the poncho over you and I'll bring you some bug spray."

Her idea sounded just plain dumb, but I wasn't thinking clearly and had no other option, unless I wanted Death By Mosquito. So I pulled out the poncho, sat down on the side of the road, and covered myself in that thin coat of plastic.

And then I prayed harder than I've ever prayed. "Please, please Lord. Please don't let a car drive by and see me sitting here." For twenty minutes, my prayer was answered. But then my fear came to pass. I heard a car coming. "Please, please Lord. Please let that be my wife."

But it wasn't my wife. A car sped by and I was more than relieved that they didn't stop and ask what in the world was going on. And then the car stopped and turned around!

"AAAHHHH!" said that voice inside my head.

A lady with a Shih Tzu on her lap rolled down her window. "Are you … okay?"

"Yes, I'm fine." I whimpered. "I'm getting eaten by mosquitoes so I'm just waiting for my wife to get here with some bug spray."

A concerned look flashed across her face, and then she drove away.

After thirty minutes my wife arrived, and saw the most pathetic scene I'm sure her eyes have ever witnessed. The person she had vowed to stay with through sickness and health was sitting cross-legged on the side of the road covered by a thin sheet of see-through plastic. I had smeared blood on my arms, legs, and face from swatting mosquitoes.

I am so thankful that my wife rescued me. She is a true angel. And I'm so embarrassed that she had to see her husband wrapped up in a plastic bag sitting on the side of the road. I wouldn't blame her if she thought of me as less of a man. Not only did those mosquitoes suck out my blood. They also sucked out some of my dignity.

* * *

On another occasion, I ran a marathon before work one morning. The idea was planted in my mind years before, when I read a blog post by one of my ultrarunning heroes, Davy Crockett. (Yes, that's his real name.) Just for fun and for a unique challenge, he woke up really early one morning and ran a marathon before work. (I remember him saying that he did this when his wife was out of town so she wouldn't be able to tell him he was an idiot.) This guy takes conventional wisdom and throws it out the window. I suppose that's why I admire him so much.

Choosing to run a marathon was a spontaneous decision. While driving home from work the night before, I thought it might be a good day to try the Marathon Before Work. I felt like my training was at a level where I'd probably be okay getting in a spontaneous marathon. Here are the steps I took to complete the Marathon Before Work adventure:

1) Start running at 1 a.m.: I needed to make sure I would finish 26.2 miles with enough time to get ready for work. Spoiler alert: When you go to bed at 10 p.m. and then wake up three hours later to run a marathon, the sound of your alarm clock might make you break out in tears.

2) Take a DEET shower: Bug spray with at least forty percent DEET for me. The mosquitoes in our area are like blood-sucking vultures, and you'll recall that I happen to be a mosquito magnet. Mosquitoes look at me like I'm a supermodel. I didn't start running until I had sprayed so much bug spray on my legs that they were glistening.

3) Cool temperatures are overrated: I live in a climate that, even at 1 a.m., resembles running in a sauna filled with molten lava. Because if it doesn't feel like you are running through a molten lava sauna, you're doing something wrong. (I maintain that it is morally and ethically wrong for a city to be eighty-eight degrees at 1 a.m.)

4) Find a good route: I ran a loop around the city that was around eight miles long, stopping back at my house twice to refill my pack with fluid and calories. I made sure to grab an ice cold can of Mountain Dew each time I stopped at the house. I also refrained from walking straight to my bed, which seemed to be saying in a sultry, alluring tone, "Cory, I miss you."

5) Have good entertainment: It could get a little boring running by yourself for hours in the dark. I had some Ultra Runner Podcast, Trail Runner Nation, and Radio Lab podcasts to keep me occupied. I still managed to get sleepy, but it's much easier to combat the sleep monsters while running through civilization, as opposed to being alone on a trail in the middle of nowhere, in the middle of the night. (Then it can be VERY hard to fight off the sleep monsters.)

6) Don't make eye contact: As the sun came up, I made sure to avoid making eye contact with passing drivers. Between the bug spray on my face and the sweat dripping into my eyes, I'm sure my eyes looked like I was crying. An advantage of running a solo marathon is that you don't have spectators lying to you, saying things like "You are almost there!" (LIE!) "You're looking good." (LIE!!) It's best to just avoid human contact. I kept a steady but conservative pace and managed to finish the 26.2 miles.

7) Now you get to go to work: Now that I had 26.2 miles on my legs and three hours of sleep, I arrived home to take a quick shower, get dressed, and head out for a full day at work. On the way to work, I made sure to make a stop at a gas station and purchase the biggest Dr. Pepper money could buy. If you decide to run a Marathon Before Work, I'd suggest you do the same. Because, yeah. You're going to need it.

* * *

Even though summer mornings are hot, they are nothing compared to the heat on summer evenings. On a sweltering evening in July, I participated in a run that was far from solo. The heat, combined with the higher than normal humidity, made the air feel like a steam room. People started showing up and parked on the streets surrounding our house. They walked to the driveway carrying their offering of high fructose corn syrup.

Hostess, with its beloved Twinkies and Ding Dongs, had gone bankrupt in 2012, shutting down operations. (There was a great deal of mourning at our house for the loss of a loved one.) But in 2013, Hostess reopened! I thought it would be fun to have a running party to celebrate the return of Hostess.

We invited friends, neighbors and their families to come over to our house and bring a treat to share with the rest of the group. My girls decorated the driveway with sidewalk chalk. Runners were greeted with gigantic cupcakes and butterflies on the driveway. Danica was particularly creative, drawing a person who had eaten too many donuts and then threw up. (Karma came back to bite her when she was up at 2 a.m. with a sick stomach. Diagnosis: Too Many Donuts Syndrome.)

Mel and I set up tables on the driveway for big jugs of water and the sugar loot. There is a one-mile loop around our house, so we ran that one-mile loop for hours with an aid station that resembled a buffet you'll find in heaven: cookies, cake, donuts, and every kind of Hostess product you could ever ask for.

People could go as fast as they wanted and do as many loops as they wanted. It wasn't a race. It was a celebration fun run. We had a blast running into the night, laughing, joking, and trying to avoid throwing up. On a Facebook post, a friend wrote, "Last night I became a member of the Church Of Hostess, and Cory Reese is the pastor."

17) Don't Talk To The Care Bears

Mastering the mental side of ultrarunning

I wanted to quit at mile eleven, when it felt like the sun was three inches away from my body.

I wanted to quit at mile twenty-two, when I had to keep stopping over and over again behind trees for bathroom breaks.

I wanted to quit at mile twenty-five, when my legs seemed to shout, "If you're feeling this crappy right now, how in the world are you going to go another seventy-five miles?"

I wanted to quit at mile thirty, when I saw the trail ahead that looked like a vertical climb into the clouds.

I wanted to quit at mile thirty-nine, when my friends Jared, Clair, and Catherine were having a fun conversation, but I couldn't contribute anything because I was too busy trying to not upchuck all over myself.

I wanted to quit at mile fifty-six, when my friends were done with their race and I headed out into the wilderness, in the dark, alone.

I wanted to quit at mile seventy, when I stood alone in the darkness and imagined that mountain lions were licking their chops in excitement as I passed.

I wanted to quit at all those times. And at least hundred more times as I ran the Ultra Adventures Grand Canyon 100. Yet somehow, I managed to make it to the finish line. Immediately after crossing the finish line, I knelt down and gave Mother Earth a sloppy, wet kiss. Considering how poorly my race went, it was virtually a miracle that I made it to the finish line.

Although ultrarunning has an enormous mental component, the physical aspect of training and race strategy can't be overlooked. I cringed at one race when I talked with a fellow runner at mile three. He said that it was his first hundred miler.

"I haven't really trained the way I should have, but they say that an ultramarathon is ninety percent mental, and I'm mentally strong so I think I'll be okay." It turns out he wasn't okay. He didn't make it half way before dropping out of the race. Though strong mental training doesn't compensate for a lack of physical training, it can certainly help compensate for physical limitations.

My finishing times tend to be slower than most. I put in sufficient training to prepare for races, but still often find myself up against cutoffs.

Despite being far from the talent of elite runners, I have tenacity and stubbornness. I've worked on becoming stronger mentally to help offset some of my physical limitations.

I've come to realize that our bodies will go as far as they need to go — and not much farther after that. If I'm going out for a ten-mile training run, my body is ready to be done running after ten miles. If I'm going out for a thirty-mile training run, my body is completely spent after thirty miles. The same thing happens in ultras. Your mind will help regulate your pace and energy exertion — as long as you don't try to override the system by going too fast.

In my training and racing, I've worked to improve on tricks that help improve mental strength:

1) Smile. Research has shown that endorphins and serotonin are released into our bodies when we smile. Why is this so important while racing? Endorphins are natural pain relievers. And serotonin has been associated with mood and the feeling of happiness. *Acting* happy helps tricks your body into feeling a little better.

So what do you do if you're in the middle of a race feeling absolutely miserable, and you have nothing to smile about? My choice is to "fake it 'til you make it." Often, Mel will meet me at various aid stations during a race. I'll see her Facebook posts a few days later and they will say things like "Cory is at mile 47 and looking good." My demeanor may be good, but many times it is a complete lie. But I'm telling you: If you stick with the smiling and optimism long enough, you'll start to actually feel it.

It's completely normal to feel bad. Ultramarathons aren't supposed to be easy! But whining and complaining won't help matters. They only keep you stuck in negativity and focused on how bad you are feeling. When you're stuck in this funk, remind yourself that you chose this. Instead of focusing on how miserable you are, focus on what it's going to take to get you to the finish line.

2) Visualize before the race how you're going to solve problems when the train goes off the track — WHICH IT

WILL. Try to envision every possible scenario and how you'll handle it. Imagine feeling worse than you've ever felt before — a sick stomach, legs on fire, exhausted, sore knees, falling asleep, blisters, etc. Then multiply that by ten. Have an action plan to handle anything that could possibly go wrong. Before my first hundred-miler, I tried to imagine the absolute worst I could ever feel. Even then, the physical and mental difficulty was harder than I imagined.

One of the things I love about ultras is that there is always more to learn. Often, the best way to learn the lessons needed to succeed in an ultra is the hard way. Having run a bunch of races, if anything could go wrong, it probably has at some point during some race. But when that happens, you have an opportunity to work through it, and you'll have more experience and confidence to handle that problem when it comes up again in the future.

3) Be willing to embrace suffering. This approach is completely opposite to the normal, everyday life we live. People try to avoid suffering. We don't want to hurt. But in an ultramarathon, suffering is normal. It's acceptable.

Ultramarathons teach you a valuable lesson: It is possible to suffer and keep going. It is possible to suffer and not give up. It is possible to suffer and become stronger because of it. This one lesson is applicable to everyday life more than anything else I've learned through running. The ability to embrace suffering has been an asset when our family experiences a trial. It has been a benefit when things are tough at work. It has helped me work through illnesses. This one tool can't be bought, but it is priceless.

4) When times get tough during a race, and your pace resembles that of a sleeping tortoise, don't stop. Martin Luther King Jr. said, "If you can't fly, then run; if you can't run, then walk; if you can't walk, then crawl; but whatever you do, you have to keep moving forward." It's almost as though he was intentionally writing a script for how to succeed during ultramarathons. Consider the title of Bryon

Powell's book on running ultramarathons: "Relentless Forward Progress." For many runners, this phrase has become their mantra during races. Don't sit around wasting lots of time at aid stations. Get in, get what you need, and get out.

5) Remind yourself of all the training and hard work you have done to get to this point. Personally, I remind myself of the months and months of getting up insanely early to get my runs in. During most of those mornings, I just wanted to turn off the alarm and go back to sleep. It's hard to get out of a nice warm bed to go run in the cold, alone in the dark, for hours before work. But I do it anyway. I remind myself of the work I've put in and think to myself, "Do I want to waste the work I put in all those mornings because the race has gotten hard?" Imagine how incredibly amazing it will feel to cross the finish line!

6) If you start hallucinating that your running partners on the course are Care Bears, leprechauns, or unicorns, don't talk to them. Just keep moving.

7) It is always darkest before the dawn. Just like in life, it can get a little ugly out on the trail. It's not always smooth sailing. But don't give up. Whatever you do, don't give up. Be patient enough to let things turn around. I have had so many experiences where I was really struggling and didn't think it would get better ... and yet it did. But you have to stick with it long enough for things to turn around.

8) If you have crew or pacers, enlist them to help in your fight. I strongly recommend talking with your crew and pacers beforehand. Give them coaching and tips about how to best help you. Do you want them to go in front of you or follow you? Do you want them to talk or just be quiet? Let them know what kind of encouragement works best for you. Though pacers and crew can be a great resource for support, when all is said and done, the only thing that will keep you going is a persistent whisper inside yourself to not give up.

9) While in graduate school for social work, we learned about the term "catastrophic thinking." Catastrophic thinking is when we get stuck in negativity, focus on worst-case scenarios, and lose hope of anything positive. The

negativity spirals into disaster. In an ultramarathon, it's nearly impossible for me to avoid catastrophic thinking at some point along the way. In talking with other runners, it sounds like catastrophic thinking is fairly common.

This is how catastrophic thinking shows up in ultrarunning: "This blister is killing me. I'm so exhausted I can't see straight. I feel horrible. I still have forty more miles to go! There's no way I'll be able to go forty more miles feeling the way I do. I'm just going to stop."

To help combat the destructive catastrophic thinking, never, ever do math while running an ultramarathon. Don't try to calculate pace and think, "I'm not going to make the upcoming cutoffs." Absolutely do not try to predict the future. Only focus on the mile you are running at that very moment, and not how many more you still have to go. I repeat: Do not think about future miles. Only focus on the current mile you're running. Don't give up, even if it seems like you won't make a cutoff. Countless runners have been up against cutoffs that probably seemed impossible to meet (myself included), but managed to find another level of strength to persevere. Let that urgency spur you to push harder instead of give up.

10) Understand that often in a hundred mile race, the last thirty miles can be as difficult as the first seventy. Plan accordingly and expend your energy wisely, especially early on in a race. Expect that you will have to dig deep toward the end of the race. You may have to search your soul for a level of strength and courage that you've never had to call on before. But it's there. Trust me. It's there.

Just because I know what to do, doesn't mean I always do it. In the middle of a race, my mind makes lots of justifications, and lots of excuses about why it's okay to quit. Actually implementing these tools in the middle of a race can be easier said than done.

One clue that you need an immediate mental course correction is when you start thinking about how you're going to explain why you dropped out to your family and friends. If you begin to formulate your Facebook post explaining why you needed to drop out of the race, that should be your notice that the red warning light is flashing. DO NOT LISTEN when your mind starts making up justifications for why it's okay to quit.

Not a single one of these tricks is the magic bullet. Often, it takes a combination of many of these tools to get to finish line. Mental strength takes time and experience. Have faith that you have what it takes to succeed. Believe in yourself and your abilities. The most important characteristic you can have is a willingness to do whatever it takes to finish. As Ken Chlouber, founder of the Leadville Trail 100 said, "You're better than you think you are. You can do more than you think you can."

18) When You Get Caught On Ultrarunner Candid Camera

Thoughts on DNFs

I am a firm believer that you can accomplish whatever you put your mind to. But what happens when "whatever you put your mind to" is to finish a race, before that race kicks you in the crotch and leaves you whimpering and writhing in pain, and you don't accomplish what you put your mind to? In ultrarunning, there is a three-letter word that strikes fear in the hearts of everyone who has the courage to stand at the starting line: DNF. Those three nasty letters stand for Did Not Finish — the racing equivalent of being kicked in the crotch and left whimpering and writhing in pain.

My thought is that if you're taking the risk of doing something as monumental as running a marathon or an ultramarathon, sometimes things aren't going to go your way. It's inevitable. You aren't a true ultrarunner until you've dreamed mighty dreams, given all your effort in a race, and then had those hopes and dreams exploded by a truck full of dynamite. I've had a few of those proverbial kicks in the crotch from races. I have a few DNFs under my name.

In 2012, I returned to the scorching desert trails of Arizona to run the Javelina Jundred again. At this time, I had two hundred-mile finishes behind me. I was confident that my experience earning those two buckles, plus my training, would leave me well-prepared to tackle the race and earn a third buckle. You know what they say. "Confidence killed the cat." Or at least that's what the saying should be.

I felt like I was on Ultrarunner Candid Camera the whole weekend. Anything that could possibly go wrong, did. The mishaps actually got to the point where they were really funny. I look back now and think, "Did all that stuff really happen?"

Strike 1: I knew it was a bad omen when I walked into a gas station before the race and heard Bette Midler's song "Wind Beneath My Wings" playing. You need to be seriously careful about what is going through your head at the start of a race. Because whatever is tumbling around your skull will be stuck on repeat over and over and over again when you are out alone on a trail hour after hour. "Wind Beneath My Wings" was absolutely not the kind of upbeat tune I wanted to get stuck in my head before a long, long race.

Strike 2: The Javelina Jundred is a race and "Jalloween" party. Lots of people dress up. Knowing this, in the month before the race, I racked my brain for a costume I thought would be both funny and capable of sticking with me for a hefty dose of miles.

One night, Mel came home with a bag in her hand. "Here, I found you a costume for Javelina!" I opened the bag and saw a clown outfit that should in no way be worn by a grown adult. It was a silky, long-sleeved, long pants jump suit that tied in the back.

"Wait. What? No. I'm not wearing this at Javelina." But she insisted. "It will be perfect! I have some big glasses and a clown wig you can wear with it." Since I didn't have any better ideas, I hesitantly relented.

A little bit of my manhood died as I stood at the starting line wearing that clown outfit. It occurred to me that I looked like I was wearing a Hazmat suit with polka dots. And I was starting to sweat even before I started running. I quickly realized that my costume resembled an oven. It was like being baked into a Hot Pocket. Experts say that you should never try something new on race day. I recognized that this advice included wearing a Hot Pocket-like clown costume.

Strike 3: The costume virtually required an act of Congress to take it off if, say, you need to go to the bathroom. Bad. Really, seriously bad. It didn't occur to me until after I started running that there was no escape route with the costume if, say, you need to go to the bathroom. If it so happens (and it did so happen) that you need to go to the bathroom, you need to take off your hydration pack and wrestle with the strings on the back of the clown suit to get the stupid thing off. Go ahead. Try untying a series of six knots on your back in forty-five seconds or less. I'll skip the details, but let's just say this almost proved to be highly tragic. No bueno.

Before the sun came up, it was already getting warm — even for runners who weren't wearing a clown costume. We knew we were going to be in for a hot day. I ditched the clown costume after fifteen miles — that was the best part of the race. Things steadily progressed downhill after that.

By the time I had run ten miles, I realized I may have a bit of a problem. My stomach did not feel good at all. This was early in my ultrarunning experience, when I was using primarily sports gels (essentially one hundred calories of sugary slime packed into a little foil wrapper). In previous long runs, my stomach didn't get to this point until my mileage hit the seventies. I was a little concerned, but there was no sense in stressing about it. I just kept moving forward waiting for things to work out.

The funny thing is that after thirty miles, things still hadn't worked out with my stomach. Any time I tried to eat something, I became even more nauseated. A few times while eating a gel packet, I threw up in my mouth but instinctively swallowed it again. And that is really disgusting. I'm sorry. That was probably too much information.

We had reached the hottest few hours of the day (around eighty-seven degrees, maybe a bit hotter out in the middle of the desert) and I could see that the heat was getting to some of the runners. Let's just say it wasn't unusual to come across a chunky pile of liquid on the trail. There was not a solitary cloud in the sky and no shade anywhere on the course. It's a good thing I abandoned the costume after fifteen miles, otherwise I would have ended up as a melted pile of clown on the side of the trail.

I was so thankful when I saw the moon come up and knew that the temperature would start dropping soon. My stomach still felt sick and I hadn't eaten more than a few gel packets for eleven hours. After forty-five miles, I was still moving well, but I knew my lack of calories would catch up to me unless something turned around soon.

As the sun went down, I whispered a quiet prayer telling God I'd be psyched if my stomach would start to feel better so that I could eat something and be able to continue the race. But I also agreed that if this prayer wasn't answered the way I wanted, I wouldn't complain and I'd be thankful for the experience. I hoped that the setting sun would give me new life. Despite feeling crappy, I wasn't giving up.

The next loop from miles forty-six to sixty-one were in the dark. I loved hearing coyotes howling at the moon. It was a psychological sucker punch to the gut to look at mountains far away on the horizon and see little pin pricks of light. I knew those pin pricks of light were headlamps, and that my feet would have to carry me there.

My stomach deteriorated from bad to worse. It was now at the point where even taking a drink of water made me gag. To prove how bad my stomach felt, I'm a bit of a junk food junkie in everyday life, and the aid stations had *everything* a runner could possibly want: pretzels, chips, different cookies, brownies, pumpkin pie, candy, noodles, soup, tortillas, pizza, sub sandwiches. Everything. And during my entire twenty-four hour race I ate: one gummy worm, four pretzels, two ginger snaps, and five M&Ms.

Houston, we have a problem.

Mel had volunteered during the day at an aid station, so she was worn out and exhausted. She planned to get a bit of sleep, then come out to pace me at mile seventy-six. But when she saw me come in to Jeadquarters after sixty-one miles, she knew I wasn't doing very well and decided to join me for the next lap instead of waiting until later. That's when the night got really crazy.

Mel told me that earlier in the day at the race parking lot, someone backed into our rental car, made a big dent, and drove away. The thought of paying a five-hundred-dollar deductible for something so dumb made me frustrated and helped contribute to the negative frame of mind I seemed to be stuck in.

And then, out of nowhere, we saw a coyote fifteen feet ahead of us on the trail. Mel was petrified. I, on the other hand, was too exhausted to care. We saw it run up the ridge, then look down at us with its glowing, beady eyes. Mel was freaked out but I reassured her the same way I did the first time I ran Javelina. "You don't need to outrun the coyote, you only needed to outrun me. And that shouldn't be too difficult right now."

Don't forget the fact that we were on Ultrarunner Candid Camera, where if something could go wrong, it would. About an hour later, Mel's nose started bleeding. It was gushing blood. And of course we happened to be absolutely nowhere near an aid station. So we hung out on the side of the trail to do some first aid on her middle-of-the-night-bloody-Niagara-Falls ailment. Eventually it stopped bleeding. Yet again, it was so unfunny that it was funny.

After an actual eternity, we finally reached the next aid station: Jackass Junction around mile seventy. Since I couldn't eat, my brain was fuzzy and my muscles were fried. I knew that if I didn't hurry, I wouldn't make the time cutoff at the next aid station and would be pulled from the race. I didn't care. I hoped I wouldn't make the cutoff. Instead of hurrying, I laid down on the ground for a little while to stretch. In the meantime, Mel had laid down near the drop bags because she was so tired that she was sleep walking too as we went down the trail.

My feet and quads felt thrashed but we made the final push to Jeadquarters. After a while I said, "Are we going the right way?" Mel said to chill out. She thought I was hallucinating. But I didn't see any footprints in the dirt. We then realized we took a wrong trail. I'm embarrassed to admit this because Javelina course markings are perfect. Someone could be blindfolded and not get lost here. But we managed to take the wrong trail. After turning around we saw that we walked right past a "Wrong Way" sign. Dumb.

I got back to Jeadquarters after twenty-four hours and twenty-four minutes, and seventy-seven miles (or seventy-eight if you count our detour). I didn't make the cutoff to go on to the next lap so my race was over. Out of the 364 runners who started, only 160 finished one hundred miles. I was so grateful that the episode of Candid Camera was over.

I made some obvious errors in the race (not the least of which was that Godforsaken clown suit). An ultramarathon is a long time to be running. If you make a few mistakes, you have plenty of time to identify them and get back on track. But if you string too many of them together, it makes arriving at the finish line very difficult. Obviously the Hazmat suit should have stayed home. I should have had a backup for nutrition if my stomach went south. I wasn't aggressive enough at combating sleepiness during the night, and when that sleep monster grabs hold of your back and starts suffocating you, it's hard to get him off. It's best to just keep the monster off in the first place. Mel felt bad that she didn't make the situation any better because she was so tired as well. It ended up being a bad combination of events — and an excellent learning opportunity.

* * *

In 2015, I collected another DNF at the Jackpot Ultra Running Festival. A few months prior, Mariah Carey performed a Christmas song on television. The song started off tune and became progressively worse, ending in a fiery train wreck of off-key notes. Jackpot became my own personal Mariah Carey performance. Things started off on the wrong foot and I was never able to get the train back on the tracks.

In the weeks leading up to the race, I wasn't sure if I was going to go for a hundred miles. I was signed up for the hundred-miler but considered dropping down. My knee had been feeling tight and I didn't want to make things worse. The race is in Las Vegas, where crappy buffets abound and one out of three residents is a fake Elvis.

The absolute highlight of the race was running with Mel and Jackson, who both signed up for the twelve-hour race. (There were options for six-hour, twelve-hour, twenty-four-hour, and hundred-mile races.) Years ago, I had this fantasy about running Jackson's first marathon with him when he got older. At that time I didn't expect that he would be shooting for a marathon at age thirteen. And yet he decided the marathon distance would be his goal for the twelve-hour Jackpot run.

It had been a few years since Mel ran her last marathon, and she swore that she would give birth to a baby rhinoceros before she'd run another. But at Jackpot, she decided she would shoot for finishing a marathon also. Jackpot is a good place to do something like that because the race directors really go out of their way to help runners succeed. (Read: brownies at the aid station.)

I pretty much knew from the beginning that it wasn't going to be my day. Within the first few miles I was channeling my inner Mariah Carey. I decided to just have fun, talk with runners, and take what the day gave me. That year, Jackpot was on Valentine's Day. Mel and I spent it together with a couple hundred other people. Running. And sweating gallons by the hour because it was 8,613 degrees outside. And eating cheesecake at the aid station. And waiting for each other at the porta-john. And commiserating about achy legs. It was super romantic.

I kept plugging along at approximately the speed you move when standing in line at the DMV. My knee and body didn't want to cooperate. I admit, it was frustrating to be going so slowly, particularly because the course is so runnable and smooth.

I managed to compound my not-so-great situation by accidentally stubbing my big toe on a big rock. I'd like to describe to you how it felt. Years ago, Mike Tyson fought Evander Holyfield. In the middle of the fight, Tyson bit Holyfield's ear off. Remember? Well, after I kicked that rock, the rest of the race felt like Mike Tyson's teeth were clamped onto my toe. And Mike Tyson's teeth are sharp! (On a related note, a few days later I only had nine toe nails.)

I was so impressed watching Jackson during the race. He didn't whine or complain at all during the times I saw him. He just kept moving forward. It was an incredible feeling to talk to him later in the race when his mileage continued to build and I knew he would reach his goal. He is determined and stubborn — the two most important characteristics of runners.

We had the misfortune of running on a day that set a record high for Las Vegas. It reached eighty degrees — about twenty degrees above average. For February, that's pretty warm. I kept my shirt soaked in water all day and kept ice in a bandanna around my neck, which helped keep the heat manageable. One minor side effect of a wet shirt and dripping bandanna is that your shorts get a little wet too, and it looks like you drank a gallon of Gatorade and didn't make it to the bathroom in time. Worth it? Definitely.

I decided that I would stop at fifty miles. I had some big races coming up, and didn't want to be sidelined. This decision didn't come easily. I wrestled back and forth for hours. It can be discouraging to not accomplish what you set out to do. But an ultramarathon isn't supposed to be easy. When you attempt something so challenging, there is always a risk that it won't turn out quite as planned. Unless you are always playing it safe and never challenging yourself at races, DNFs are almost always part of the territory.

As the sun went down, I was so inspired by my fellow runners. I was impressed with so much positivity, encouragement, and determination.

For example, I spent a bit of time with my friend, Mark Mccaslin. He said he was having a rough day and not feeling good at all. A few minutes later, he barfed up what looked to be a thirteen-course meal. And yet he finished one hundred miles! I am constantly amazed that amidst difficult conditions and personal challenges, people persevere.

So I went on to finish fifty miles. But this story has a remarkable ending. Mel and Jackson didn't just finish a marathon at the Jackpot Ultra Running Festival. They both kept going after 26.2 miles and each of them finished a 50K (thirty-one miles) — their first ultramarathons! I can't express how proud I was of them. To be able to watch them along their journey was such an amazing experience. They did their last lap together. Despite my race going about as crappy as possible, that was far outweighed by the awesome ending to this adventure.

"Believe that you can run farther or faster. Believe that you're young enough, old enough, strong enough, and so on to accomplish everything you want to do. Don't let worn-out beliefs stop you from moving beyond yourself." ~ John Bingham

* * *

Later that year, I went to the Bryce 100 to pace my friend Jared Thorley, who was going for his first hundred-mile finish. Jared had paced me through many miles at many races, and I was eager to begin to repay the favor. I was also thrilled to spend some time on the trails surrounding Bryce Canyon National Park. If you haven't yet experienced the beauty of Bryce Canyon in Utah, put down this book, throw some clothes in a suitcase, and go. Now. It is arguably the most beautiful place on earth.

I planned to meet Jared at the fifty-mile point, make sure everything was going okay, and then ride with his wife to the sixty-mile point and run the last forty miles with him. This plan allowed me to enjoy the most awkward shuttle ride ever. Imagine this:

I'm in a school bus. There was only one other guy being shuttled to the fifty-mile point. There was the bus driver. He was just a young kid. And his assistant (or copilot?) was an older, clearly unrelated lady.

He grabbed his phone and started a play list on the radio. Then these two kind souls sang Josh Groban songs as we cruised down a dirt road for an hour. Nope. Not a joke. I plead the fifth on whether or not I joined them on a rousing version of "You Raise Me Up."

I waited at the fifty-mile point. And while I waited, I chatted with ultrarunning legend Hal Koerner. All of the ladies in ultrarunning have a crush on Hal. (And if we're being completely honest about this, so do all of the guys.) But it wasn't just Hal I talked with. I also visited with elite runner and freak of nature, Timothy Olson, who had won the Western States 100 for two years in a row. They were hanging out there because their wives were both running the race. This made my day.

Jared's expected arrival time came. And went. A half hour passed. Then an hour. And then another hour. By the time Jared arrived, it was cold and dark and he was flirting with cutoffs. I was concerned. I knew from previous conversations that Jared wanted this race badly. I decided I wouldn't wait until mile sixty to join him, I'd start at mile fifty. He grabbed some food at the aid station, and then we plunged into the darkness.

Jared was struggling. His legs felt like they had been lit on fire. Everything hurt. Every ounce of energy had drained out of him. Then the most incredibly peaceful, awe-inspiring sight opened up before us. We saw the moon looking so brilliant and gigantic rising over the horizon and we both stopped dead in our tracks to take in this beautiful sight. It was stunning.

Keep in mind, the Bryce 100 course is brutal. It is certainly one of the most scenic places I've ever run, but the trails are incredibly difficult. He made up a fun game to distract himself from his painful legs. The game was called Name That Fluid. When we passed a wet part of the trail, Jared would try to name the fluid. Barf? Urine? Blood? We saw all of the above on the trail.

The reality of the situation gripped Jared, and he knew that he wouldn't be making the next cutoff. So when his legs could take no more, we'd sit on the side of the trail for a minute with our headlights off, staring at a canvas of a trillion stars above us.

At mile sixty, Jared's race was over. I knew the feelings he was having. I know that realization that I gave the best I had, but my best wasn't quite enough. I've been there, done that, and bought the T-shirt. I hate that T-shirt. That feeling really, really sucks.

In the days following that race, I thought a lot about that feeling of failure and the frustration that comes from not finishing a race. I wanted to try to articulate that getting a DNF (Did Not Finish) at a race is NOT failure. Here are five truths about a DNF:

1) Just clicking the "Register" button for a race shows epic faith and determination. Countless people think these races are cool, but they are too scared to pull out the credit card and make a commitment to run. You were brave enough to take that risk.

2) Running is a gift. I work in a healthcare setting with chronically sick people who would kill to be able to run. We are blessed to be able to do this. So whether you make it three miles or eighty-nine, we are so blessed to even be out on the trail.

3) Consider this from Theodore Roosevelt, who said, "Far better is it to dare mighty things, to win glorious triumphs, even though checkered by failure ... than to rank with those poor spirits who neither enjoy nor suffer much because they live in a gray twilight that knows not victory nor defeat." Just showing up at the starting line proves that you "dared greatly."

4) Valuable lessons can be learned when things don't work out as planned. I despise hearing that kind of crap after I've "failed," but after a little time has passed, I can see that every single time I have collected a DNF it has been a valuable learning opportunity, and I have bounced back smarter and stronger. There are lessons learned through a DNF that you can't learn any other way.

5) Let that "failure" light a fire under your rear end. Ramp up your training. Add some miles to your week. Run another hill. Eat an apple instead of a glazed doughnut. (Just

kidding — pretend I never said that.) Make your legs burn. Push out of your comfort zone. Strengthen your mental determination. Do a speed workout. And most importantly, CLICK "REGISTER" FOR ANOTHER RACE so you can KICK SOME BUTT!!!!!!

19) Set It And Forget It

Running a sub-twenty-four-hour hundred-miler, 2014

When I first started running, I would "race" when I ran races. I began each race with a goal finishing time and pushed as hard as I could to meet that goal time. Sometimes when I raced, I hit my goal time. But often I didn't. After failing to meet a goal, there was always at least a small part of me that felt disappointed. Driving home from a particular race where I didn't meet my goal, I felt disappointed in myself. Then it was as though a hand slapped me across the face when I realized how absolutely foolish it was to feel disappointed in myself. After all, I had just run 26.2 miles!

Now, when I hear people say they feel discouraged or disappointed in themselves for not meeting a goal even though they worked as hard as they could, I feel sad. I want to shake them and say, "Hey, do you know how incredibly awesome it is that a human being can actually run 26.2 miles? And what's even more awesome is that you — YOU — ran 26.2 miles! Be proud of yourself!"

Over the years I have come to realize that it's okay to have a goal finishing time. But a fast finish isn't the only worthy goal. Most of the time that I run races now, my goal isn't to finish with a certain time. My goal is to have a ridiculous amount of fun. I assure you that during a hundred-miler, there are times when your body is really, really grumpy. And having a ridiculous amount of fun can be a really, really hard goal to achieve. But generally I enjoy striving for that goal more than I enjoy striving to achieve a certain pace or finish time.

That isn't to say that I never try to finish with a faster time. In 2014, I decided on the Jackpot Ultra Running Festival as a race that I wanted to actually race. Prior to Jackpot, I had hundred-mile finishes that ranged everywhere from twenty-seven hours to thirty-five hours to finish. I really wanted to push myself to see if I was capable of finishing a hundred-miler faster than twenty-four hours.

The Jackpot Ultra Running Festival is held on a 2.3-mile loop through Cornerstone Park in Las Vegas. People ran that 2.3-mile loop over and over and over again until they hit one hundred miles. This was the first time I had ever run a short-loop course.

I knew that the area was fairly flat. I'm a firm believer that race-specific training is one of the biggest keys to success when preparing for a race. I knew that I needed to train my body to run flat miles as opposed to the hilly trails and mountains I was used to running on. I also needed to train my mind to zone out and get accustomed to running for hours without the distraction of awesome scenery around me.

So to train for the race, I ran hundreds of miles at the local middle school track. This had the added bonus of being a dirt track, which was a little easier on my legs. I would regularly complete twenty-mile training runs on that quarter mile loop. That race-specific training certainly came in handy on race day.

The night before the race, I laid there trying to visualize myself feeling good during the race. In my mind's eye, I saw the race going well and finishing before the clock hit twenty-four hours. I did my best to get a good night's sleep. Which is to say that I didn't sleep at all.

I had been using Tailwind Nutrition as my running fuel for years. Before the race, I mixed up gallon jugs of Tailwind and kept them in a cooler next to the race course. My plan was to only stop long enough during the race to fill up my water bottle when needed. In and out. No dilly dallying. Keep moving forward. Livin' la vida loca. Ice, ice baby. I believe I can fly.

The race course circled a small lake full of ducks and geese that honked incessantly like broken bike horns. Every 2.3-mile loop took us past the main aid station, complete with chips, candy, soda, brownies, and cheesecake. From an outside perspective, this sounds like heaven. Christopher McDougall's book "Born To Run" (mostly) jokes that a hundred-miler could essentially be considered a jaunt from one aid station buffet to the next. Ultramarathons play a cruel joke on runners who arrive at a buffet of food which would have looked scrumptious before the race. But in the middle of the race, the food looks unappealing at best, and vomit-producing at worst.

I remember seeing an infomercial years ago for a rotisserie cooker. The audience kept chanting, "Set it and forget it!" For some reason that saying popped into my head while I was running. I really focused on staying in the "set it and forget it!" mindset during the race. I got into a steady pace where I was pushing but not overdoing it, then stayed there. Hour after hour. In the zone. Just livin' la vida loca. (Thank goodness *that* song didn't get stuck in my head for a hundred miles!) That got me to the fifty-mile mark in ten hours and thirty-seven minutes. I was ecstatic. I had never run fifty miles that fast before.

When I reached fifty miles, my friend Marcellus Assiago showed up to pace me for a while. I was starting to bonk a little bit before he got there, so I hoped I could get back on track. Marcellus is a Kenyan runner who has finished a marathon in a nauseatingly fast two hours and forty-eight minutes. This was his first encounter with an ultramarathon. On my first loop with Marcellus, I showed him the easier parts of the course where I pushed, and the harder parts of the course where I held back. (There weren't any particularly "hard" sections of the course, but late in a race, molehills become mountains.) I wanted him to just lead me along. Set it and forget it.

For the four hours he paced me, I focused on nothing but his rear end by the light of a headlamp. We talked very little. It was exactly what I needed. Some runners like their pacers to be chatty and talk a lot to take their mind off their angry legs. For me, trying to hold a conversation takes too much mental energy when I'm exerting all my focus into putting one foot in front of the other.

After about twenty miles, Marcellus left and my plan was to just hang on and try to make sure the wheels didn't come off the bus. I very desperately wanted to run a sub-twenty-four-hour race. Whenever I started to feel discouraged, tired, frustrated, or exhausted, one number popped into my head: Twenty-four.

I wasn't wearing a Garmin watch and didn't really know what my pace was. But as the sun started to rise on the second day, I realized that if I kept setting it and forgetting it, I may be able to achieve the inconceivable sub-twenty-four.

I got to mile ninety, and could taste that sub-twenty-four. I think it tasted even better than the cheesecake they were serving at the aid station in the middle of the night. I started to push even harder. I was so excited knowing that unless the wheels really fell off, this was going to happen.

With four miles left I broke down crying. It was the same emotion I felt when I neared the finish line of my first hundred-miler. I've always felt kind of inadequate as a runner. I always thought it would be impossible for me to finish a hundred-miler faster than twenty-four hours. I would have never, ever believed it. And now it was about to happen.

I stopped before I got to the finish line. I wanted to breathe in every bit of this experience. The impossible happened. Twenty-two hours and twenty-five minutes. And I was at the finish line. That feeling of shock and happiness is one I will never forget.

20) Fueled By Hostess

Solo hundred-milers, 2014

In February 2014, I was looking at a calendar of upcoming races for the year. I had a good collection of hundred-mile races that I was planning to attempt. I realized that if I ran all the races I wanted to run, and then added a few more, I would be able to run a hundred-miler per month for a year.

I ended up achieving that goal, and in the process saw some of the most beautiful scenery in the country. I watched the sun rise over the Great Salt Lake during the Antelope Island Buffalo Run. I climbed and descended mesas and slickrock on the outskirts of Zion National Park during the Zion 100. I experienced my own insignificance in the universe as I stood on the rim of the Grand Canyon during the Grand Canyon 100. I saw brilliant autumn colors covering steep mountain peaks during the Bear 100. I listened to coyotes howl at the moon in the Arizona desert during the Javelina Jundred. My final two hundred-milers ended up being part of the same race when I finished the first hundred miles at the Across The Years seventy-two-hour race on December 30. Many hours later, I finished one hundred and five more miles by the time the race ended on January 1.

I loved those experiences and cherish the relationships I built with people during the races. But some of the highlights of the "Hundred Miler Per Month" year came when I ran solo hundred-milers. I needed a few hundred-mile runs during some months when there weren't any races close by. I also wanted to try something different and challenging.

I didn't know anyone who had done a solo hundred-mile run before, so I didn't have anyone's brain to pick for ideas or suggestions going into my first solo run. I had a base of nine hundred-milers in the past, but I figured I'd choose a location where it would be easy to bail out just in case something went wrong.

I decided on a route from the Utah state capitol building along State Street in the heart of Salt Lake City, fifty miles south to the city of Provo, and then turn around and come back. I would finish the run back at the capitol building.

I feel very conscious about wanting to make sure my running isn't a burden on anyone. I didn't want to ask Mel to follow along for a hundred miles to provide aid. That sounded like the most boring job ever, and I didn't want to put someone through that. I wanted to be self-sufficient and not rely on others to finish the run. I named the run the Hostess Hundred because:

1) Hostess products are delicious;
2) I didn't want to take myself too seriously with all this stuff;
3) The Hostess raspberry-filled donuts are delivered straight from heaven on the wings of angels.

I planned to use gas stations for my aid stations along the way with at least a fair amount of calories coming from Hostess products. I mistakenly believed that if Twinkies taste so good, surely Twinkies would taste so good while running a hundred miles. (It turns out this wasn't remotely accurate.) I didn't plan ahead of time which gas stations to stop at, as I figured I'd just make stops as needed.

I planned to do the run completely solo. I love running by myself and do ninety-nine percent of my training alone, so I wasn't concerned about being alone during those hundred miles. Not to mention the fact that I was surrounded by a city full of people. It's much harder to feel alone while running through the streets than it is when you're by yourself in the middle of the night on a trail without another human being in sight.

I have some friends in northern Utah who run, so I posted online the route I was planning just in case anyone wanted to join for a few miles. When I arrived at the state capitol on the morning of the run, I was met by Becca Wood and Robert Merriman, who suggested that an adventure like this needed to start with a jumping picture. I wasn't hard to convince.

Within the first two miles, we were joined by two running legends: Matt Van Horn and Jennilyn Eaton. Both had won the Antelope Island Buffalo Run a few months prior. Usually, you'd be more likely to see Sasquatch eating bacon and eggs at Denny's than to see these two mountain runners doing some miles on the road. I was honored to have their company.

Jennilyn said, "Do you have a SPOT tracker so people can track your progress online?"

I told her that I didn't have a tracker. The thought never crossed my mind.

"Okay. Let me make a few calls. I'm going to find one that you can carry for the rest of the run. We'll share the link so friends can follow your progress."

And as if the party couldn't get any better, we were joined by Renee Yeoman, who was training for her first ultramarathon, and Cherri Marcinko who won both the Salt Flats 100 and the Grand Canyon 100 recently. It's safe to say that I felt a bit overwhelmed by all the speedy runners surrounding me. But I felt completely humbled and thankful for their company.

We were laughing the whole time and may have (okay, did) make a quick stop at 7-Eleven for Slurpees. They ran for many miles before leaving me to do some running on my own. Jennilyn found me shortly afterward and clipped a SPOT tracker to my pack.

"There. We can track you now!" she said. "Good luck! You're doing awesome!"

It was scorching hot outside, and I got a bit behind on electrolytes. My legs started cramping up, but I knew it was something I could work through. I felt like a Kentucky Fried Chicken dropped into boiling oil.

Suddenly I heard a car honking behind me. Then some cheering. It was Mel and my daughters, who tracked me down to say hello and cheer me on. The soft breeze of the air conditioner when they rolled down the window felt amazing. Mel said, "Here, do you want some of my Diet Dr. Pepper?" Moments later, I looked down and realized that I accidentally had half of the contents of her mug in my stomach. Oops.

I ran alone in the heat for an hour before a van pulled up next to me, driving slowly. He watched me for a minute then sped ahead and pulled into a parking lot that I was approaching. I cautiously proceeded when suddenly a man wearing running shorts got out of the van.

"Hi, I'm Wan Kou!" he said. He told me he heard about the run and asked if I'd like some company for a few miles. Of course I welcomed the companionship.

"Oh, I brought you something," he said. He went back to the van and pulled out a large box of twenty Twinkies. "Here, I know you like Twinkies. You can eat these!" At the moment, my stomach was a bit edgy because of the heat. I knew it was a distinct possibility that I might throw up if I ate a Twinkie. But I was so touched by his kindness.

My sweaty fingers fumbled to open the package before eating one Twinkie. I told him that was all I could eat for now. He glanced at my hydration pack with enthusiasm. "You can put the rest of them in there!" I knew there wasn't a prayer that I'd eat nineteen more Twinkies but I opened a pocket in my pack and shoved them inside. Wan joined me for ten miles in the worst heat of the day before turning around to run back to his car.

We neared the top of a hill, and I could imagine my shoes melting to the pavement if I stood still too long. There was a white truck parked at the top. When I got to the truck, Kendall Wimmer, who I only knew from Facebook, got out.

"Hey Cory!" He had a cooler full of ice to fill my water bladder with. He had bottles of ice-cold water. And he gave something more valued than ice on a hot summer day. He gave encouragement.

A few miles later, I passed another Facebook friend, Scott Wesemann. I had followed his athletic achievements and knew that both he and Kendall were accomplished runners. When I saw each of them, I had feelings of insecurity creep into my head. "I'm moving so slowly compared to how fast they are. I'm walking more than they would ever walk in a race. Maybe they'll think less of me as a runner."

But as we talked, I didn't get the slightest hint that they felt this way. They were completely supportive and encouraging. I got the feeling that they genuinely didn't care one bit about the fact that I was so much slower than them. I was again reminded that we tend to be way harder on ourselves than anyone else is.

After Wan left, I stopped at 7-Eleven again to refill my hydration pack and restock on some calories that weren't cream-filled sponge cake. Snickers: check. Swedish Fish: check. Mountain Dew: check. As someone who is more than a little bit of a germ freak, I can think of few things more disgusting than the mouth piece of my hydration pack bladder sliding against the top of the gas station counter while refilling my back. And that is precisely what happened. I was completely grossed out.

My cousin Kody Nelson lives in the area and came out for a few miles. Kody isn't a runner. Which wasn't a problem at all, because at that point I was going through a slump. My energy was waning and my legs were achy. I was happy to just be moving forward at a fast walk. That stretch had very little running. As we walked, we caught up on family, and work, and I did my best to formulate an answer when he asked how I called what I was doing "fun." We are two nuts that have fallen from the same tree.

Evening finally arrived, and it started to cool off a bit. My body functions great in the cold. Not nearly as great in the heat. So I was ecstatic that it wasn't quite as hot. I had been eating a steady diet of junk food all day to get the calories I needed. But Snickers and Swedish Fish can only suffice for so long.

I was starting to feel hungry for real food and decided to make a quick stop at Subway. They were incredibly busy and incredibly slow. I stood there patiently in line watching the minute hand of my watch tick forward. I could have watched the entire movie "Titanic" while I waited. But while I stood in line, I met Steve and Adrienne Parsons, who were following my SPOT Tracker and wanted to say hello. They insisted on buying my sandwich. I was so thankful for their kind gesture that I could have hugged them. I decided against it after remembering that I was in the middle of a hundred-mile run and was covered in sweat.

After Kody departed and I had a Subway sandwich in my possession, I ran alone for a mile before a bicycle pulled up beside me. It was my friend Susette Fisher, who I was able to run with a few months earlier when she completed her first hundred-mile race at the Jackpot Ultra Running Festival. She rode her bike next to me for a while as we talked.

Right as Susette finished up, I was joined by my friend Catherine Kalian. We stood on the sidewalk admiring the incredible sunset. I told them, "That sky looks like it has been Photoshopped." It was simply beautiful. Catherine spent many miles in the dark with me as we pushed to the fifty-mile turnaround in Provo. There was a gas station at the turnaround where I bought a lemonade for each of us. I was much more careful with the mouth piece of my hydration pack this time when I refilled it with water.

Literally one minute after Catherine left, a car pulled up and a few guys hopped out in running clothes. This was the most amazing part of the entire run. It was as if a bunch of friends and soon-to-be-friends had a secret meeting before this run and decided where each person would join me so that people wouldn't overlap and I'd have company for almost the whole run.

The guys who hopped out of the car were Sam Jewkes and Jeff Davis. I've run many of the same races they have, but had never talked to them because, well, they're fast, and we were never at the same part of the race course. I had a total blast talking with these guys and getting to know them better. They made those miles float by, which is saying something when you are fifty-five miles into a run.

It was the middle of the night when they left and it was time to get more miles on my own. For me, the demons generally start creeping in around mile sixty of hundred-milers. In order to run one hundred miles you need to get comfortable with doubt, fear, pain, and loneliness. Eventually things are going to get ugly and you start to wonder how you'll be able to take another step, let alone go forty more miles. Everything — EVERYTHING — hurts. This difficulty and doubt is something that I could never begin to truly understand until I was around mile sixty of my first hundred-miler and I realized that one hundred miles was harder than I had ever imagined. You must continue to put one foot in front of the other. Nobody can do it for you. It's all on you.

I try to stay positive and smile, even if it's the opposite of how I'm feeling. I try my best to prevent that darkness from continually tightening its grip on me. Negativity and whining don't make anything better. I appreciated those miles alone to work through the challenges.

I passed one fast food restaurant that still had its lights on: Del Taco. I saw that although the restaurant was closed, the drive-through was still opened. "Crap!" I thought, remembering how I had been turned away at Wendy's when I tried to walk through the drive-through at night years earlier.

I sheepishly walked up to the drive-through window. I played the "I'm running a hundred miles" card. With a look of desperation I said, "I know you're only supposed to serve food to people in cars but I've been running for sixty-five miles and I'm starving. Is there any possible way that I could buy a few tacos and a Coke?"

The guy at the window looked over at the cook as if to say, "Should we do it?" The cook shrugged his shoulders. "Yeah, we'll make you some tacos." I again resisted my urge to hug a random stranger and happily walked down the sidewalk alone in the dark enjoying three glorious tacos.

It was still pitch black outside when I saw another car stop ahead of me. Two girls got out of the car and joined me for many miles until finally a hint of sunlight started to appear above the Wasatch Mountains. Those girls were Cherri and Renee, who ran with me on the first day and returned for more miles.

After Cherri and Renee left, I had another chunk of miles alone. (I'd estimate that over the entire hundred miles, there were only maybe thirty to thirty-five that I spent by myself.) With the sunrise, the heat returned. I laughed to myself as I thought, "You know, I could be at home laying in my bed right now watching 'The Price Is Right.' But no, I had to go run a hundred miles."

I had some new companions join me as I was pushing toward the last stretch: Monte and London Riding. I first met them at the Jackpot Ultra Running Festival. I wished I could have run faster with them, but my legs had other ideas. Then Jennilyn met me on a street corner with a sandwich and some fresh strawberries. I was touched by her simple act of kindness.

As we crested a hill, I got my first view of the state capitol building far in the distance. It seemed a million miles away. (Which was strange because I knew that the whole run from start to finish was quite a bit less than a million miles.) I worked on staying focused on the mile I was in instead of how far there still was to go. With about ten miles left, I did get some pep in my step when I started smelling the barn.

Then something positively wonderful happened. Sam Jewkes, who ran with me the night before, was the band teacher at Hillcrest Middle School. As I neared that area, I could see a large group of kids at the front of the school, playing their instruments and cheering. Sam had his whole band out there. I was speechless. I was so touched. I gave them each a high five and thanked them for coming out. They were so awesome. It made my day.

I had some great support in the last few miles as I neared the capitol. Wan stopped by on his lunch break and did the last few miles with me in his work clothes. I met DJ Loertscher, who came to run the last stretch with me. Zac Marion from Altra brought me a cold towel he had kept in ice as he waited for me. And Catherine left her school class to join the last few miles. And finally — FINALLY — I arrived at the state capitol one hundred miles later.

My family was waiting at the capitol building when I finished the run. I felt incredibly indebted to all those running angels disguised as my friends who came out to support me. Between the stops to refill my pack, grab food, and wait at a bajillion stop lights, the entire run took almost twenty-eight hours.

I had planned to do this run solo. But it turned out to be far from solo. I got emotional thinking about all these amazing people who were coming out to support me. I didn't know why they were doing this, but I was so humbled and touched by everyone who came to run a few miles with me, or met me along the way to give me ice, or just to stop and say, "Good job." It meant so much to me. If I could have scripted the perfect experience for my first solo hundred-mile run, this would have been it.

* * *

Coming up with a hundred-miler the next month, July, was tricky. There weren't any hundred-mile races remotely close to home. I considered the possibility of running on some of the hundreds of miles of trails and roads around my house. The problem was the temperatures in southern Utah in July, which regularly top a hundred degrees. In the spirit of not being a burden to anyone on my runs, I didn't want to ask my wife to follow me around to various trailheads to provide food and water. I could park my car at a trailhead where I could do out-and-back mileage coming back to my car when needed to refill water in my pack. But with temperatures at a hundred-plus degrees, I'd only be able to get a few miles out before I'd need to turn around and head back for a refill.

I tried to think of any possible way to get a hundred miles in while not traveling out of state, not burdening others, and taking into consideration the southern Utah heat. Then a thought came to my mind: a hundred miles at the high school track. Granted, a hundred miles on a quarter-mile loop could potentially be mind-numbingly boring and unlike any running challenge I had ever done before. But doing a hundred miles at the track would allow me to be self-sufficient. I would never be too far away from water. My friend Shelly Thomas was a teacher at the high school. She got permission for me to run at the track for a few days. She also managed to get me one of the most important things for doing a hundred-mile track run — a key to the bathroom.

I started running at 4:45 a.m., when the temperature was still hovering at eighty-two degrees outside. It wasn't long before I saw my first sunrise of the run. I've always tried to model my life after the sage wisdom of wise, poetic, pasty-white musician Vanilla Ice and his lyric, "Ice, ice baby." (I'm allowed to call him pasty white. Takes one to know one.) I hoped an ample supply of ice would help get me through the run.

I planned to be completely self-sufficient and brought all the food and liquid I figured I would need for the run. It was also comforting to know that home was only a few minutes away, so if I got in a bind, I could always call Mel and have her bring something if needed. I brought three coolers with tons of ice (ice baby), water, and soda. For snacks I had Fig Newtons, chips, candy, and gallon jugs of Tailwind that I mixed the night before.

Once at the track, I found a hose that I soaked myself in every few laps. This ended up being a blessing and a curse. Keeping myself wet was the most important thing that allowed me to keep running in the heat. I would wet myself (that just sounds wrong) and then be completely dry two laps (a half mile) later. So I'd wet myself again. (Not that kind of "wet myself".)

The problem was that this also completely soaked my shoes, so I had a case of Sloshy Shoe Syndrome for literally sixty miles. After the run, my feet looked like a chewed up Big Mac. My feet had to enter mental health therapy to deal with post-traumatic stress disorder when this one was over. But in all seriousness, running with soaking wet shoes for sixty miles was positively agonizing.

I was willing to have permanently wet feet in exchange for staying a little cooler. With no control over the temperature, I just dealt with wet shoes. But I tried to get everything going in my favor that I did have control over. This basically boiled down to my attitude. I had learned by now how important it was to stay positive and focus on the mile I was running instead of how many more miles I still had to go.

There is an electronic marquee in front of the high school that is viewable from the track. It would show a few upcoming school activities, then flash the time and temperature. I watched the hours slowly pass by on the marquee. With each passing hour, the temperature climbed until finally topping out at a hundred and seven degrees. I'd imagine that this is what it feels like to run inside a fireplace. In Hell.

I tried to keep my eyes from glancing over at the temperature on the marquee. It didn't help my progress at all. In fact, mentally it made the run more challenging because it gave validation to the negative thoughts that kept creeping into my mind. That marquee was like passing a bad car wreck on the freeway. I didn't want to look. And yet I couldn't turn away.

I hit a rough patch in the late afternoon. The track was radiating heat and it felt like I was standing under a hair dryer. But every once in a while a friend would stop by and say hello or bring a little treat, which lifted my spirits. Melanie Roberts brought a banana and Hostess donuts. Michelle Ennis brought a smoothie. Matt Anderson brought a Slurpee. Angel Johnson brought a popsicle. Lyle Anderson brought a smoothie. Shannon Gardner brought some sandwiches from Arby's. Katrina Judd brought a Slurpee and some candy. Leif and Melissa Burton stopped by to make sure I was still alive. Lyle came back and brought a cookie and the most delicious substance known to mankind: "Dirty Dr. Pepper" (Dr. Pepper with a shot of coconut syrup.) I never asked a single person to come and visit. I never solicited any treats. But all these people came anyway. I felt so touched by their kindness.

From the track, I could see Smith Mesa on the horizon. Smith Mesa is part of the Zion 100 course. The steep ascent to the top of the mesa sends runners climbing a thousand feet into the sky in less than a mile. I gazed longingly at that mesa in the distance. In my mind's eye, I could see the incredible views of southern Utah from the top of that mesa; views that were, unsurprisingly, quite a bit more scenic than the quarter-mile loop I was spinning around.

In the evening, Mel and the kids came over to share a few laps with me at the track. For a few minutes, I almost forgot about the huge temper tantrum that my legs were throwing. Mel said, "You're kind of hurting right now, aren't you?" I didn't want to complain or let her in on my rough patch because I didn't want her to worry about me.

"Well, I don't know. Why?" I asked.

"You have your hands on your hips. Whenever you're really hurting during a race, you always have your hands on your hips." I looked down and realized she was right. (Since then I've been more aware of my hands-on-hips posture during races. Mel's observation was, indeed, accurate. It seems to be an automatic response when things start to get ugly. Some people cry when they're going through a dark place. Some get angry and throw tantrums. I put my hands on my hips.)

My dad always said, "Patience is a virtue." I loathed that phrase when he used it, because it was always when I wanted something RIGHT NOW. But in an ultramarathon, few things are as important as remembering that patience is a virtue. I've learned that when times get really tough, you just have to be patient because things will get better. It's guaranteed that at some point, things will get really ugly. But if you hang in there, it will get better. I knew if I could make it through the heat of the day, I'd feel better when it started to cool off. I was rewarded with a sunset flaunting a kaleidoscope of colors, a gradual drop in temperature, and even a few droplets of rain. My son Jackson begged to stay at the track with me for the night.

"Why would you want to do that Jackson?" I asked. "You would get so bored."

But he insisted that he wanted to stay. "I'll just walk around the track while you run."

I didn't see any harm in letting him stay. I figured when he got tired, he could just go sleep in the car. "Okay, you can stay." That little creature ended up getting in thirteen miles before going to the car to sleep! I admire his determination.

Once it got dark, my friend Jess Jensen showed up to run a few miles with me. Jess paced me the first year of the Zion 100 when the race took me thirty-five hours and temperatures also resembled a fireplace in Hell. She has seen me at my absolute worst. By this point in the run, I wasn't moving too quickly, but she was patient and happy and energetic.

Many years before this run, I read the book "Ultramarathon Man" by Dean Karnazes. He talked about how one night he went out for a run that was so long that he ordered a pizza to eat while running. At the time I simply could not fathom how it was possible for a human being to run for so long that they would need to eat a mid-run meal. Fast forward to five years later, when I found myself circling a high school track in the middle of a July night. It was almost midnight and I was around seventy miles in. My stomach was growling. Jackson woke up and came back to the track to walk some more. Right before Domino's Pizza closed, Jackson and I figured we would pull a Dean Karnazes and ordered ourselves a pizza.

I decided to completely disregard the time that was ticking by on my watch. I wanted to sit on the bleachers surrounding the track and just enjoy the moment of hanging out eating pizza with my son … in the middle of a hundred-mile run. I recognized that this whole experience was something I would look back on and smile. I wanted to enjoy every moment of it. Sitting on the bleachers eating pizza at midnight with my son was my favorite part of the hundred-miler. I posted a picture of this on Facebook, and was surprised when I saw that Dean had shared this picture on his Facebook page.

From about mile seventy on, the run was very difficult for me. My legs were so sore, I was so tired, and every step was a challenge. Words can't describe how daunting and humbling it is to be at mile seventy, feeling so beyond exhausted, and knowing that you still have potentially another *nine hours* (and a hundred and twenty laps!) to keep going. That is a dark time. Literally and figuratively. I got a little bit of a boost when the sun started to come up. And speaking of that — how crazy is this sport where you see *two* sunrises during the same run?

The last ten miles were silent, alone in my little pain cave. Members of the high school girls' soccer team began arriving at the field, as they had the morning before when I started running. I'm sure that when they saw me still circling the track, they probably thought, "Gross! That guy is wearing the same exercise clothes that he was wearing yesterday when he came to run!" I'm sure they had no idea that I had been in perpetual motion (aside from a welcome pizza break) for more than twenty-four hours.

By this point, I had started running the straight parts of the track and quickly walking the curves. Every step was so hard, but I wanted to keep moving as fast as I could to get it done. Just keep putting one foot in front of the other.

Mel and my daughter Kylee came by to visit on the second morning. I kept thinking about how awesome Mel is. A few weeks before the run, we were sitting in church. I leaned over to her and whispered, "I think I want to try running a hundred miles around a track."

Instead of saying, "You are an absolute lunatic!" she said, "When were you thinking to do it?" Her response was completely casual and unquestioning. I might as well have been asking if she wanted to go to Dairy Queen for an ice cream cone. I felt so thankful for her support and encouragement.

Kylee wanted to run the last mile with me. I told her she didn't need to do that, but I was so happy that she insisted. Finally after twenty-six hours fifty-five minutes, I finished one hundred miles at the high school track. A few people commented that this sounded so miserable. Of course, at times, it definitely was. However, I figured that "so miserable" was code for "excellent mental training for upcoming adventures."

The heat was by far my biggest hurdle. When I finished, I felt completely demolished. It felt as though I had sweated out every last drop of fluid in my body. There was no jumping celebration at the end of this run. My worn body crumpled into the grass on the field and I laid there gazing at the clouds as the sound of a soccer game echoed in the distance.

* * *

A month later, on a Thursday afternoon in August, I found myself hobbling into a Jimmy John's sandwich shop in Cedar City, Utah. As I opened the door to walk inside, I imagined that parents would shield the eyes of their onlooking children; staring at how pathetic I looked, covered in too many layers of sunscreen, bug spray, and sweat. This 100 mile adventure ended at a sandwich shop. But it started two days earlier on trails around Navajo Lake in southern Utah.

Sometimes I wonder if I'm a glutton for punishment. (Case in point: I once ate not one but *two* McDonald's breakfast burritos … and regretted that decision for the next nine hours.) In keeping with being a glutton for punishment, I registered for the Bear 100, which was coming up a month later. Bear is a high-altitude race, so I assumed it would be advantageous to do some training in an area where oxygen is nearly absent from the air. I decided that the August 100 miler would be done at Navajo Lake — 9,042 feet above sea level, which matches elevations on the Bear 100 course.

I had never been on the trails around Navajo Lake. I didn't have a specific course laid out, and figured I'd just explore the trails in the area and see where my legs would take me. My route began on the Navajo Lake Loop Trail. It wasn't very technical or rocky, and the views of the lake were remarkable. I came around a densely forested section of trail and heard rustling on a tree above me. I looked up to see a bald eagle fly across the lake and into the distance. This is the only time I've ever seen an eagle during a run, and the beauty of the moment gave me chills.

I wasn't used to the thin air. It felt like trying to breathe through a straw while my lungs were filling with lime Jell-O. I worked on convincing myself that struggling with the altitude was a good thing. It would be good experience and training for Bear. I reminded myself that it was okay to suffer.

My car was parked in a central location that branched off in various directions to different dirt roads and trails. After looping around the lake, I ran to the nearby Virgin River Rim Trail. I didn't see a solitary person the entire time I was on the trail. I was just running down the trail, minding my own business, when all of the sudden there was a really loud rustle in the bushes right next to me. In that split second I thought to myself, "So, this is how it's going to end? I'm about seven milliseconds away from becoming a light snack for a mountain lion." I involuntarily let out the loudest, sissiest yell that has ever escaped my mouth. I guarantee if Mel heard me make that sound, she would file for divorce. Fortunately the animal that came out of the bushes wasn't a hungry mountain lion. It was a startled turkey and her flock of babies. This experience nearly left me in a situation where I would need to run back to the car to change my shorts.

The Virgin River Rim has more technical climbing, and more closely resembles the Bear 100 course. Periodically views of Zion National Park open up on the horizon, though most of the time my views were confined to the immediately surrounding forest.

I realized within the first thirty miles that this run would not proceed as smoothly as hoped. My legs felt like they had nothing to give. It was probably caused in part by the altitude, the accumulated miles over the last few months, and just having an off day. The bottom line was that my legs were fried way too early into the run.

After exploring much of the Virgin River Rim, I returned for another trip on the Navajo Lake Loop. There are sections of the trail that weave through fields of lava rock. So much of the trail is very runnable — unless your legs are fried and have no interest in running.

In the days leading up to the run, I wondered, "What am I going to do to keep my mind occupied during a long day, a long night, and probably part of another day while I run alone through the mountains?" I downloaded the audio book "Unbroken" by Laura Hillenbrand and listened to all fourteen hours of the book. I was moved by the story of this World War II prisoner of war, Louis Zamperini. Whenever I felt like what I was doing was really hard, I remembered challenges Zamperini had faced. Finishing the book left me feeling inspired and I welcomed a renewed vitality … which lasted for at least a quarter of a mile.

As the sun began to set, a wave of despair and frustration settled over me. "This is the lowest I've felt in a long, long time," I thought. I kept doing the math over and over and over in my head. I realized that at the pace I was keeping, I would have time to read "War And Peace" at least four times in the amount of time it would take me to finish a hundred miles. (Doing math in your head, and adding up how many more hours you have to go is NEVER a good idea. It only leads to discouragement.) I just really, really wanted to give up.

With each passing mile, discouragement increased. As much as I tried, I couldn't pick up my pace. The harder trails earlier in the day left my legs feeling like they were being pressed against a barbecue grill. I couldn't stop thinking about excuses to stop. I could think of a hundred valid, legitimate reasons to stop. But I only had one reason to keep going: I knew I would be disappointed in myself if I quit.

Within hours of the sun going down, wind picked up and the temperature dropped. I watched grand lightning storms far off on the horizon, both ahead and behind me. "Please, God. Please let this lightning storm move closer so I will be forced to stop my run," I prayed. When I finished the prayer, I repeated it. Then again. And again. I wanted an excuse to quit that didn't involve me giving up. But the lightning didn't move closer and I was left alone to continue running under a canopy of billions of stars.

The second sunrise of the run seemed to reward the effort I'd put in to get through the cold night. The sky was so blue, and the clouds glowed with many shades of yellows, oranges, and reds. I had now covered eighty miles, a distance I couldn't have imagined reaching the day before, when he was struggling mightily.

Morning turned to noon. Noon turned to afternoon. By this point, my hundred-miler looked less like a run and much more like a refrigerator trying to escape from quicksand. I reminded myself that even though I was really struggling, I was having "fun." A hundred-miler is fun in the way that people think riding a roller coaster is fun. They wait in a long line for forty-five minutes, have someone strap a seatbelt way too tight around their groin, they go up and down steep hills that propel stomach bile into their throats, get whiplashed to the point of needing a chiropractor — and then call it "fun." So, yeah, hundred-milers are a blast!

I completed the solo Navajo Lake 100 after thirty-one hours and fifty-seven minutes. In the twelve hundred-mile runs I had completed previously, only one had been slower. At Navajo Lake, my finish was not marked by crowds of people cheering on runners. There was no medal or belt buckle. No finish line food tents. (Unless you count the Oreos and Dr. Pepper I had stashed in my car.) There was only the sound of gusting wind and the internal satisfaction of knowing that I didn't give up.

21) Choose Kindness. Choose Patience. Choose Love.

My connection with Robin Williams

f I'm being completely honest, I don't think about my dad every day. Life is so busy that sometimes I go quite a while without thinking about him. But in August 2014, I was thrust back into all the emotions that I experienced as a fourteen-year-old boy.

I was listening to the radio in my car when I heard a news story that Robin Williams had taken his own life. Like so many others, I felt my own little connection with the amazing actor and comedian. Not too long before this announcement, I gave my kids their introduction to "Mrs. Doubtfire." "Patch Adams" gave me a new perspective on my career. And I couldn't tell you how many times I've watched "Dead Poets Society."

It seemed all the more heartbreaking that not only did he pass away, but he committed suicide. It didn't seem real. Williams didn't seem like a person wrapped in chains of depression. He seemed like your funny, down-to-earth next-door neighbor.

The reason I felt so connected to this story about Robin Williams was because that's how my dad was, too. On the outside he was the funny, personable, happy neighbor who got home from work and then immediately stopped in the driveway to play basketball with his kids. But below the surface, my dad was wrapped in those same heavy chains of despair and depression that reports say Williams had experienced. The funny, outgoing exterior covered up a sadness on the inside that was largely triggered by a multitude of health problems. Hearing about Robin Williams brought me back to that cold January afternoon when despair overtook my father.

I hope what I'm about to say doesn't imply that I think suicide is okay. It has a lasting impact on everyone left behind. But I can understand how people get to that point, because I saw it firsthand. I witnessed that smothering despair in someone I loved. I saw the feeling of being in a deep hole with absolutely no way out.

It probably goes without saying, but that day my dad died changed me forever. I soon realized that I faced a choice: I could let that action destroy and ruin me, or I could, as much as possible, learn and grow from the experience. I decided on the second option. Here is how my life has been different:

1) I think it increased my empathy. I try to understand people better. I try not to judge. I try to support and encourage. I have lots of room for improvement but I'm trying.
2) It impacted my career choice. I'm a clinical social worker and work with the belief that I can make a difference.
3) It put things in perspective. If I'm having a bad day or going through a challenging time, I always remember that it could be worse. I choose to believe that this life experience made me stronger.

So with all that said, my hope would be this:

Choose kindness.

Choose patience.

Choose love.

I'm not implying that if we hold hands and smile, everything will be fixed. I'm saying that we can never know the demons someone may be facing. Appearances aren't always what they seem. We don't know the quiet struggles someone is battling. So you and I should work on spreading kindness. A little happiness could go a long way. In a world of so much sadness and pain, show love. Shine.

It's easy to judge someone else's actions. But I can attest that seeing a loved one struggle with (and ultimately surrender to) depression will give a different perspective. The fact that Robin Williams took his own life is proof that no matter how much awesome and how much funny and how much talent someone is filled with, depression is powerful. And if those chains are starting to wrap around you, tell someone. Let someone help you. The world needs your shine.

The day that Robin Williams died, I strengthened my resolve to run a hundred-miler when I turned thirty-eight years old. My dad died when he was thirty-eight. I wanted to do something for my dad that his health prevented him from doing himself. I wanted to run a hundred miles to honor him.

22) Running On A Crisco-Covered Slip-and-Slide

Bear 100, 2014

I almost got barfed on by a stranger. I ate a Snickers bar while standing in a flash flood. I prayed that I wouldn't get struck by lightning. I got mud in my underwear. I helped people keep going when they wanted to give up. Later, they helped me keep going when I wanted to give up. I saw God's fingerprints in the beauty around me. You know, just your average ultramarathon.

In September 2014, I ran the Bear 100, the hardest race course I'd ever started. This race scared me. As I drove up to northern Utah the day before the race, I felt more nervous than Milli Vanilli before an acoustic concert. I knew more than twenty-two thousand feet of climbing would certainly get my attention. On paper, the elevation profile of the race looked like the up and down cardiac rhythm on a medical electrocardiogram machine.

The only thing that the first climb was missing was some Caribbean music playing in the background, because the first couple of hours were simply one long conga line up the steep mountain. The trail was too narrow to pass or be passed, so we all held our spots in the formation.

Once the sun started to rise, I realized that my eyes would be in for a treat. With the autumn colors, the mountains looked like they were glowing. The mountainsides were bursting with brilliant shades of yellow, and it looked as though we were running through a forest fire.

The high temperature for the day reached eighty-eight degrees. Everyone was experiencing that "Uh oh, my skin is melting" feeling. By mid-day the heat was taking its toll, and I started hearing about people getting sick and dropping out of the race. I would arrive at aid stations and see runners hunched over, barfing. From the very beginning, I worked hard to keep my pace conservative and not go out fast. Frequent stops to take pictures of the amazing scenery helped keep my pace under control.

I continued to keep my pace steady. Ninety-nine percent of the time, that is the way to go. Although looking back on this race, I wished I would have gone against that logic and pushed harder early in the race. The weather got so hideous later that it would have been better to have more miles behind me.

The thing I focused on most during this race was staying in the moment. I didn't keep track of pace. I didn't focus on how many more miles. I didn't look at the elevation chart in my pack to see what was coming up. I just wanted to run the mile I was in. It's hard to keep your brain from doing math and thinking, "Oh my gosh. I still have sixty miles to go. If I keep this pace it will take me approximately nine bajillion more hours to finish." I worked to stay focused only on the mile I was running.

As the sun began to set and the temperature cooled off, I caught my second wind. The weather reports leading up to the race said an enormous storm would hit during the race. It was coming. Not if, but when. In the evening, aid station workers had concerned looks. They were tightening down the hatches and securing supplies that may get blown away in the wind. "The storm is coming. We are going to get pounded. It's not if, but when," I heard a volunteer say.

At mile forty-five, I met a trail angel named Jenn Swanson. My friend said Jenn was looking for a runner to pace, so I met Jenn and her awesome family at mile forty-five. She would join me for the next thirty miles. She lives in the area and was familiar with the trails. I had heard of runners getting lost on this course, so I was grateful to have someone with me who knew where she was going and could prevent me from taking a wrong turn. She truly was a lifesaver.

Around mile fifty, the "not if but when" storm hit, and it hit with fury. Rain fell in currents. Wind gusted fiercely against our bodies. Thunder and lightning cracked nearby. I asked another runner, "Do you think they'll cancel the race if this gets much worse?"

"Nah," he said. "It's no big deal." It should be noted that at the very moment he said, "It's no big deal," the trails we were on had turned to rivers.

Earlier, we had tried to avoid walking through the streams to keep our feet from getting any wetter than necessary. But now those streams turned to rivers. There was no sense in trying to avoid the water anymore. It was everywhere. Inches of water covered the trails. It was weather of Biblical proportions.

As we were trudging through the water, I began to envision the elevation profile of this race. The one that looks like a cardiac rhythm.

The elevation profile that shows how the trails of this race appeared to be either straight up or straight down. Those climbs and descents became dramatically more difficult with the downpour of rain that turned the mountains into slick trails of Crisco. Hour. After hour. After hour. More rain.

I couldn't begin to guess how many times I ended up slipping on the trails. But with the rain and steep Crisco, a slip didn't just mean stumbling but then regaining balance and continuing onward. Slipping meant that our legs completely flew out from under us and we found ourselves staring up at the rain as we lay in the mud. This adventure was making the challenges on Survivor seem like a game of hopscotch. This was turning into a twelve-hour mud wrestling competition with a mountain.

It was so absolutely horrific that it was comical. I couldn't help but howl with laughter as my fellow runners and I kept ending up laying on the trail covered in mud. It was like being on a vertical, Crisco-covered Slip-and-Slide. I deeply regret that I was covered from head to toe in mud. Because otherwise I would have pulled out my camera and taken a video of this absurdly funny scene, and then won $10,000 on America's Funniest Home Videos.

My pacer Jenn was positive and optimistic. We talked the whole time, and she got me through very difficult miles. Words can't begin to describe the conditions we went through. Just when we'd think, "Wow, it can't get worse than this," the rain would start pouring even harder. It was just funny. Part of me felt so bad for putting Jenn through this experience. But she seemed to be having so much fun that it helped relieve some of the guilt I was feeling.

At mile seventy-five, we met up with my brother Kenny, who planned to pace me the last twenty-five miles. I tried to talk him out of it. "Kenny, it is so miserable out there. You don't have to do this. You can just go home and enjoy a day with your family. The runners out here are crazy. We're barely second from the left on the evolution chart."

I told him that the race had become less like running and more like skiing. Skiing on Crisco. (And have you ever tried to ski *up* Crisco before? No bueno.) But he was undeterred. With a smile on his face he said, "I'm coming with you. This is going to be awesome!" It was his first taste of ultramarathons, and he was excited.

Those twenty-five miles with Kenny were incredibly challenging as well. I was soaked to the core and freezing. I never thought about quitting, but I was scared that with the trails in such poor condition I might not be able to go fast enough to make it to the finish before the thirty-six-hour cutoff. Kenny and I pushed forward mile after mile. Although this was his first taste of ultramarathons, you wouldn't know it. He paced like a pro. In those twenty-five miles, he saw runners at the absolute lowest of lows. But they persevered. They kept going. It was such an inspirational, triumphant, and beautiful experience, seeing what people were going through. I felt truly honored to be among the runners who kept putting one foot in front of the other even when it was really, really hard.

There were many times when I wasn't sure how I was going to make it to the finish line. I went through my share of highs and lows. But finally after thirty-four hours and thirty-two minutes, my eyes saw something just as wonderful as the hundred miles of autumn leaves on those mountains: the finish line.

Even after the finish, water continued to pour from the sky. I discovered that a post-race meal at the finish line was quite a bit less enjoyable when my feet felt as though they had been standing ankle-deep in a cold swamp for sixteen hours.

The Bear 100 is an experience I will never forget. I am thankful that it was ridiculously hard, because it made me stronger. I get chills thinking about what transpired in those thirty-four hours. I will never be the same. (And by "never be the same," I'm referring to the post-traumatic stress disorder that is triggered every time it rains now.)

23) The Tale Of The Three Unwise Men

Developing and executing a successful race strategy

I 've learned some valuable lessons about race strategy. Nearly all of those lessons were learned the hard way, when I really screwed up something. It's one thing to have someone tell you to start a race slowly so that you can conserve your energy for later on in the race. But that message gets burned deep into your soul after repeatedly running races where you start out just a little too quickly, and then later explode in splendid fashion like the Hindenburg lighting up the night sky.

For illustrative purposes, allow me to share the Tale Of The Three Unwise Men: Runner Edition.

I met the Three Unwise Men while running the Bear 100. We had plenty of time to become acquainted in the first twelve miles of the race. We were together on the straight climb up the mountain for twelve miles. Like I said, this section was like being in a fun conga line. For hours. But without the Caribbean music. (And technically speaking, without much of the fun.) And instead of people downing shots of alcohol, they were downing shots of Salted Caramel Gu.

When you're in an hours-long conga line, it's fun to talk with other runners. I was next to the Three Unwise Men, so we talked about some of our favorite races. I found out that the Three Unwise Men were all friends and planning to run the whole race together. And I learned that for each of them, this was their first hundred-miler.

In those steep climbs there was almost no running. It was so early in the race that it would be foolish to exhaust your energy with ninety more miles to go. But do you know who was doing some running? Yep. The Three Unwise Men. I could hear them panting and out of breath. Not smart. Unless you're in the highest level of elite runners, you never, ever want to be out of breath with ninety more miles to go.

They got to the first aid station before me around mile ten. I grabbed a drink and a few pretzels and went on my way. Soon afterward, I reached a long, steep descent. As steep as the climb had been going up the mountain, the drop off the other side of the mountain was just as sharp. I ran alone for a long time. And then I heard runners coming up behind me. It was the Three Unwise Men. They must have spent quite a while at the aid station. They were now barreling down the trail as fast as they could go to make up lost time. The exact thought I had as they screamed past me was, "Those guys aren't going to finish the race. They are destroying their legs. This isn't going to end well." I hoped I'd be wrong.

At mile thirty, I was gaining ground on three runners ahead. One was walking like Frankenstein. The others were shuffling uncomfortably as though every step was rubbing coarse sandpaper on the inside of their thighs. As I got closer, I saw that it was the Three Unwise Men. I passed by and asked if they needed anything. I never saw them again for the rest of the day and learned that they all dropped out of the race.

The Three Unwise Men made some really dumb mistakes. Within the first twenty miles of the race, they completely ruined their chances of finishing the race. I'm not putting them down at all because I have made those same mistakes and many, many others numerous times. One glance at the chapter about DNFs will show some of the many foolish errors I have made.

I am far from being an expert. I still have so much to learn. But after finishing a chunk of races, here are some tips I've learned that apply to racing, whether you're running a half marathon or a hundred-miler:

1) Pace yourself. Trust yourself to move at an uncomfortably slow pace early in your race. It is so hard to be patient and hold back at the start when everyone else is speeding by in an adrenaline-filled frenzy. But patience in the beginning will pay enormous dividends later on in the race. I once attended a presentation by Bryce Thatcher, founder of UltrAspire hydration packs. He said that race pacing should be like spreading peanut butter across a slice of bread while making a sandwich. When you have peanut butter on your knife, you don't want to start spreading the peanut butter thickly at first and then run out before reaching the end of the slice of bread. But you also don't want to spread the peanut butter thinly at first and then have a big clump of peanut butter at the end. You want your slice of bread to be spread evenly with peanut butter. If you're running a perfect race, your energy and effort should be spread evenly throughout the entire race.

In the early stages of a race, ask yourself, "Is it realistic for me to be going this fast the last ten miles of the race?" If your answer is, "There's no way I'll be able to run this fast toward the end" — slow down. Conserve your peanut butter.

One of my most memorable experiences happened during the 2012 St. George Marathon, when I paced very conservatively early on and was able to go fast at the end. In the last seven miles, I passed 436 runners and was passed by only two. (Chip timing can show cool stats like that.) It was an unbelievable feeling to be going so fast at the end of a race instead of doing the marathon death shuffle for the last seven miles, as I had done many times before.

2) Be aware of where you are at in the race. In a hundred-miler, I make an effort to never let myself get out of breath for at least the first thirty miles. That is a long time to be patient. In that time I also never, ever bomb down hills at full speed. Don't blow up your knees and quads when you still have more than half of the race to go.

3) Bank energy, not time. In my first marathon, I felt so good in the first ten miles that I went faster than my planned pace, thinking that if I was feeling good I might as well bank some time for later in the race. That brilliant strategy resulted in a ten-mile death shuffle. It would have been much smarter to bank energy instead. I have never been in a race situation where trying to bank time early had a good outcome.

4) Be smart at aid stations. I first heard this little nugget of wisdom from my friend Ryan Anderson. Nothing can pile on minutes (or hours) to your finish time like delays at aid stations. When you're nearing an aid station, make a mental checklist of what you need to do or grab. Then when you get to the aid station, be quick and purposeful. Unless I'm stopping to dump out dirt or rocks from my shoes, I try to never sit down during a race. This is a strategy I wholeheartedly believe in … though often, this is much easier said than done.

Heed the sage ultramarathon wisdom, "Beware the chair." When I arrive at aid stations late in a race, usually what I want more than anything is to sit down and rest. My legs are aching, I'm physically and mentally exhausted, and I just want to sit. When I do sit down, it feels absolutely wonderful. I can even hear choirs of angels rejoicing. But eventually I have to get up. Eventually I have to start moving again. And when I do start moving again, I immediately go back to achy legs, screaming feet, and exhaustion. Sitting rarely makes any of that stuff better. So save the wasted time and just keep moving forward. Grab what you need from the aid station and then leave.

During the times I do sit down to rest, I will look at my watch and say, "Okay, you have exactly two minutes to sit. And then you have to get up and get going again." If you have a pacer, let them be the disciplinarian and make sure you don't sit too long. At one race, my pacer Danny was being almost tyrannical. When I tried to linger too long at aid stations, he kicked me out.

"Come on man, this isn't a coffee shop. Get out of here! Hate me now, love me later." I did hate him then. And I loved him later.

5) Treat each training run and each race as an experiment. Learn from your mistakes and do something different next time. It's almost certain that once you get one problem figured out, a different problem will pop up. That is one of the things I love about this sport. There is always more to learn. I've talked to many ultramarathon veterans who have significantly more experience than I have. It gives me comfort when they say that even with all their experience, they are still trying to figure things out and they still have more to learn.

6) Our bodies are incredible pieces of machinery. As long as we take care of them, they can take us far. One key aspect of this is taking care of our feet. Find shoes that keep your feet happy. Experiment with socks. Try different kinds of lubrication to prevent and treat blisters. I implore you to purchase the book "Fixing Your Feet" by John Vonhof. After doing a bunch of races, I thought I understood foot care. My mind was completely blown after reading this book. I realized that I only knew a small fraction of the tools for preventing and treating foot issues.

7) Give your pacers and crew explicit instructions before the race. Do you want them to go ahead of you or behind you? Do you want them to avoid conversations, or talk and try to distract from the uncomfortable feelings your legs are likely experiencing? When I have a pacer, I prefer to have them go ahead and set a reasonable pace for me. I tell them that if I'm keeping up, they are allowed to speed up a little bit. And if I fall too far behind, they should slow down. I generally avoid talking too much with my pacer. Late in a race, it seems to take all of my mental focus to simply continue putting one foot in front of the other. Trying to keep up a conversation drains my mental energy.

Before the race, think about what kind of motivation works best for you. Some people want to be pushed and challenged by their pacer. For some, a drill sergeant-like pacer is annoying and demoralizing. I strongly encourage you to have a conversation with your crew and pacer before a race about the mental and physical challenges you are likely to face. Let them know that they may see you suffering, but that's okay. Be clear on your expectation that you are going to finish the race. Emphasize that unless there is a legitimate injury or risk of injury, they should not support you dropping out of a race. Being tired is not a legitimate reason to drop out.

8) Stay focused on nutrition and hydration. It is so easy to get behind on these things, and once you get behind, it's hard to catch up again. Do plenty of experimentation during training to figure out what works and what doesn't work for you. And after you find a form of fuel that works for you, experiment with a few other backup ways to take in calories, in case your original plan goes off the track.

9) You (yes, YOU!) are capable of so much more than you know. Think about what you would want to accomplish if you had no limits. Now go DO IT! You can. It's okay to be scared. But challenge yourself to live big. Take a step beyond that line of what is comfortable. Do something your grandchildren will brag about. Turn off the television. Get off the couch. Go out and do something awesome. Because you (yes, YOU!) are awesome!

24) Inspiration From The Man With The Cowbell

Hurricane Hundred, 2014

M y hometown of Hurricane, Utah, is bursting with incredible trails and incredible views. Depending on which direction I drive when I hop in my car, I can be at a trail with smooth singletrack, or a steep, rocky mountain, or red cliffs within ten minutes. If a trail runner died and went to heaven, heaven would look a lot like southern Utah.

I have fallen head over heels in love for my adopted hometown. With an abundance of trails all around, I knew it would be easy to cover a hundred miles worth of trails if I wanted to do a solo hundred-miler in the area. So in October 2014, I gave it a shot. Since many of the trails were around the Hurricane area, I decided to call it the inaugural Hurricane Hundred.

I was certainly hesitant to run the Hurricane Hundred, mainly because the grueling Bear 100 was only six days earlier. But I had that streak of running a hundred-miler every month, which I had done for eight months in a row. Our family was going to be really busy in October, so if I wanted to get in a hundred for October, it had to be that weekend. I had never tried to do two hundred-milers six days apart.

Whenever I started to doubt whether or not it would be possible to run a hundred-miler per month, I thought of my friend Ed "The Jester" Ettinghausen who, that same year, was going for a World Record for the most hundred-mile races in one year. Ed finished the year with an absolutely unfathomable forty races of at least one hundred miles, including very challenging races such as Bryce, Chimera, and Badwater. Completing that many hundred-plus-mile runs in one year, Ed regularly ran races that were only a week apart.

I first met Ed while running my first hundred-miler at Javelina Jundred. By running a 15.4-mile loop in opposite directions each time, runners are regularly passing other runners going one way or another. I was going down the trail when I heard the ringing sound of a cowbell in the distance. Ahead, I saw a tall man dressed in a jester outfit: long white tights, a colorful shirt, and a jester hat. This man was carrying a cowbell during his race to cheer for other runners that passed by. "Okay, these ultrarunners are the coolest people ever!" I thought.

My friendship with Ed grew as we shared many miles together at various races. The more I got to know Ed, the more I admired and respected him. He is the epitome of encouragement and support of other runners. He is also the picture of determination and bravery by having the courage to attempt such a challenging world record. Though running another hundred-mile distance after only six days would be very difficult, Ed's example inspired me to at least try.

I started the run in Warner Valley, a spider web of dirt roads and trails that weave past bright red cliffs, fields of wildflowers, and rolling hills as far as the eye can see. But after only three miles, I considered bailing out. I just wasn't feeling it. My legs were stiff, achy, and it felt as though every ounce of energy had been drained from them. Of course it wasn't too hard to figure out why, considering the mileage from the week before.

I sat down on a rock at three miles and had a heart-to-heart talk with myself. "Should I keep going or end the streak?" The absolute top priority in all my training and racing is to keep my body in good shape and avoid injury to the extent that I avoid Katy Perry music — which is a lot.

I sat thinking for a bit and figured I'd go a few more miles before making a final decision. Finally after eight miles, my legs loosened up and I felt much better. I thought, "Maybe I can do this!"

By midday it was toasty hot, reaching eighty-six degrees. I had my car parked in a central location that branched off in different directions. I had lots of water, ice, and snacks in my car. I would stop to refill my pack every fifteen to twenty miles, which worked well.

I really, really love races because of the camaraderie and the opportunity to spend time with other awesome runners. I also really love these long solo runs. It's fun to have no specific course, no cutoffs, no aid stations, and no pressure — just running for the sake of running. Because running is awesome.

By late afternoon, I felt like someone popped me inside a microwave. The heat was zapping my energy. I kept moving as well as I could. My route included miles on dirt roads, trails, and off trail. To keep my mind occupied while out alone in the desert for all those hours, I listened to a bunch of podcasts. Some of my favorites are Ultra Runner

Podcast, Trail Runner Nation, and This American Life. Between the podcasts and the beauty of the wide desert vistas, I never felt bored.

I would have killed for a bit of cloud cover. Just a little bit of shade. But alas, there was nothing except a white contrail behind an occasional airplane overhead. Come on Mother Nature, work with me on this one!

Mel and Jackson wanted to run some miles with me, so after forty-two miles on the trails, I paused my Garmin and drove a couple minutes back into town to meet them at the middle school track. I had a lot of fun running five miles with Mel and Jack the dog.

After Mel left, my thirteen-year-old son Jackson came over to do some laps. He said he was planning to stay all night. He would run for a while then take a nap when he got tired. I agreed and it was great to have him there with me. I couldn't help but think about the time when he stayed with me all night in July when I ran a hundred miles around a track. He is a good kid.

I struggled greatly during the night. I was so tired and sore and beginning to fall asleep while running. I felt insanely jealous when I would look over at Jackson, who was sound asleep on a blanket laid across the soft grass. I desperately wanted to curl up beside him and go to sleep. Early in the morning, Jackson woke up and got some more miles in. He ended up doing a total of thirteen miles. I was so proud of him and his dedication to working hard.

After Jackson was done running, I still had ten more miles to reach one hundred. I decided to pause the Garmin again and drive a few minutes up the road so that I could finish the run on trails. I went to Gould's Rim, a trail that is a short ten minutes away, with views so beautiful that I hoped they could distract me from the fact that my legs were sobbing.

Years ago, when I was running on Gould's Rim, I found an ancient artifact called a Van Halen cassette tape. I couldn't help but laugh at the thought of someone being so upset when they realized that their Van Halen tape popped out of their Walkman when they were out on the trail. I put the tape in a secret spot and visit it every time I'm on Gould's Rim. It was still there on this visit.

After twenty-six hours and twenty-eight minutes, I finished the Hurricane Hundred — my ninth hundred-miler in my streak of running one per month. It was nearly impossible to wrap my head around the fact that my body was willing to run two hundred-mile runs six days apart. I'm just a guy who likes to eat pumpkin pie, drink Diet Dr. Pepper, and watch Major League Baseball playoff games. I'm not some kind of elite runner with a sculpted, muscular body. You only need one look at me to know that.

So what I'm saying is that bodies are amazing. We can do some really awesome stuff. It wasn't too many years ago when I gave up on my goal of running a marathon because my knees wouldn't let me get past six miles.

I'm thankful that bodies adapt. God knew what he was doing when he built us. So if you have a goal with your running, go for it! You want to go for a half marathon? Great! Do it! You want to run a hundred-miler? Sweet! Do it! Because that sense of accomplishment from running and working hard is awesome.

"If one could run without getting tired, I don't think one would often want to do anything else." ~ CS Lewis

25) Running Like A Sloth On Ambien

Wasatch 100, 2015

M el, I don't think I can drive."

My legs were shaking like a newborn giraffe trying to stand for the first time. She got into the driver's seat and I sat in the passenger seat. We drove for ten minutes in the dark, past empty street lights, through a world that was still asleep. My legs were quivering as we drove to the start line of the Wasatch 100 Mile Endurance Run in September 2015.

Exactly two years earlier, I happened to be in northern Utah and went to spectate at the Wasatch 100. I found the aid station at mile thirty-eight and cheered for friends who passed through during the race. Standing at the aid station, the heat was thick and stifling. I also followed the trail for three miles up the mountain to take pictures of runners along the course. Prior to this day, the extent of my knowledge about the Wasatch 100 was:

1) It was in Utah;
2) That it was really, really hard. But I couldn't grasp the difficulty of the course until I actually walked those three short miles of it.

The steep mountain ridges, combined with the relentless heat, were more than I wanted to experience in a race. Following that encounter, I posted on my blog, "This past Friday I had the opportunity to spend some time on the course of the Wasatch 100. I'll admit, what I saw confirmed that this race won't be going on my bucket list. I am nowhere near man enough to tackle that beast."

And yet, despite my experience that day, the race did leave me intrigued. What would it be like to run a hundred-miler that challenged me beyond anything I've ever done before? I figured I'd at least put my name in for the lottery and see what would happen. The problem with putting your name in for a race lottery is that suddenly your name has a chance of being selected. And if it does get selected, you may find yourself driving to the starting line with legs that are shaking like a baby giraffe.

I spent five months preparing for Wasatch. I went to the steepest trails I could find, and then ran them. I would do hill repeats, hiking up as fast as I could, and then running back down. When possible, I would run during the heat of the day to prepare for the impending Wasatch 100 furnace. I needed all the training I could get, because everything about Wasatch played to my weaknesses. I'm not good on steep climbs. And I'm even worse on steep descents. I don't trust my footing and I worry about rolling an ankle, so my descents are meticulous, labored, and slow. I'm not good on technical trails. Basically I'm not very good at anything Wasatch will throw at you.

My body quivered as I waited at the starting line, but once the race started, the nerves went away and it was time to focus on the task at hand. We headed into the darkness. It was a stunningly beautiful sight as I stopped on the side of the trail to look at a line of headlights weaving up the mountain and a line of headlights following behind me.

The cumulative gain at Wasatch is 25,763 feet, which is roughly the equivalent of running to the top of Mount Everest four thousand times. One particular climb early in the race had the adorable name "Chinscraper," giving runners the pleasure of scrambling on their hands and feet to the top of a steep, rocky ridge. I appreciated the spectators standing at the top of Chinscraper, who alternated between cheering and mocking runners for being so slow. Toward the middle of the climb, I looked up and thought, "Okay, where is the trail? All I see is a steep mountain of rocks and loose dirt." I took what looked to be the best way up. I chuckled toward the top when one guy yelled, "Bad line, man! Bad line! You should have angled right instead of left over there!"

For the first few hours of the race, I went back and forth with a guy who was making it hard to concentrate on the trails because of the sounds his body was making. It sounded as if he had a poltergeist in his chest that he was trying to cough out. I didn't get irritated though, because let's admit it, nobody wants a poltergeist in their chest.

When we reached the top of Chinscraper, we were able to see the valley floor and the city far below us. The city resembled the view you would see from an airplane. As the day went on, temperatures continued to climb. I had this "What was I thinking?!" moment when I realized that I was climbing insane trails in ninety-plus-degree temperatures — which is precisely what I swore I wouldn't be doing exactly two years earlier.

Living in southern Utah where the temperature regularly resembles the surface of the sun, I had plenty of heat training. And yet, I still felt like a hot dog who had sat on those rolling cookers at 7-Eleven for three days.

When I arrived at aid stations, the first thing I would ask is, "Do you guys have any ice?" I had to laugh when I hit three aid stations in a row, and at each of them their response was, "Oh, sorry, we just ran out. But I could get you some cold water." It didn't take long to realize that "cold water" was code for "water that has been sitting in a jug in the back of the truck since yesterday afternoon."

Within a mile or two after leaving the aid stations, the water in my pack felt warm enough that I could have boiled a pack of Ramen Noodles in it. Granted, it would have been great to have ice at a few more aid stations, but aside from that, the aid stations and the volunteers were exemplary. I really marveled at what a well-oiled machine the Wasatch 100 was. Every single one of the volunteers deserved a medal of honor.

From there, I experienced more miles with the poltergeist runner, scorching heat, and stunning fall colors. Late in the afternoon, my stomach was grumbling a little when I reached an aid station. I'm not sure what got into me, but I attacked that place like I was a kid that had just tasted sugar for the first time. I ate Ritz covered with peanut butter. Watermelon. Popsicles. Grapes. Swedish Fish. M&Ms. Wafer cookies. Pretzels. Twix. Animal cookies. At that moment everything looked absolutely amazing and I couldn't cram stuff in my face fast enough. Now *that* will give you a good sugar buzz!

Around mile thirty, I started to struggle with uphills. I was running downhills fine with no exertion. But the moment I started climbing, I just couldn't catch my breath. Each hill had me breathing like I had just been under water for a few minutes. It continued that way for the rest of the race. (This happens to be a little embarrassing when you're with your pacers and you are gasping for air while they are breathing just fine.)

I could tell that the heat was catching up with runners. Many looked wilted and deflated, for good reason. I got to the Big Mountain aid station at mile thirty-nine and was ecstatic to see my crew and pacers for the first time. Mel and Jackson helped crew for the whole race. My friend

Jared would pace later that night, but he stopped into the aid station earlier in the day to hang out and cheer. He brought me a Mountain Dew Freeze from Taco Bell, and then proceeded to hold it in front of my mouth and feed it to me like I was a baby bird while I changed my socks. (He didn't have hurt feelings when I politely declined the bean burritos he brought.)

My first pacer at the Wasatch 100 was my friend Clair. I am constantly amazed that even after having a couple of decades on me, this guy can still cruise down the trails faster than I could hope to. Clair joined me for miles thirty-nine to fifty-two, and we watched the last light of day turn to darkness. I was ecstatic at the prospect of the temperature beginning to cool down.

At mile fifty-two, I met up again with Mel and Jackson. They had a big pizza sitting on my drop bag. The only thing that sounded better than being at the finish line was pizza. And if one huge piece of pizza is good, two huge pieces of pizza are better. So I grabbed two huge pieces of pizza and inhaled them like a vacuum cleaner sucking up dust bunnies. Now this is going to come as a complete shock, but two huge pieces of pizza at mile fifty-two of a hundred-miler is basically a gigantic mistake. Suddenly I was the one who felt like I had swallowed a poltergeist.

It was also at mile fifty-two that my friend Jared took over pacing duties. More than anyone else, this guy was instrumental in preparing me for the race. He ran Wasatch the year before and gave me all the tips I needed. He knew exactly when to kick my butt, and when to lay off. He pushed, threatened, encouraged, laughed, distracted, and kept me moving.

I had some rough patches during the night. I hate those times when you are just overcome with exhaustion and start sleepwalking and you just want to curl up on the side of the trail and take a nap for an hour or nine. Thankfully, once the sun came up, I started to snap out of it.

At mile seventy-five, we reached an aid station at Brighton Ski Resort. The aid station is affectionately known as "The Morgue." Walking into the aid station inside the lodge, I was greeted by a host of runners in various conditions. Some had bloodshot eyes and laughed as they told their family members how crazy those trails were at night. Some runners were asleep. Some runners were hunched over garbage cans, heaving their guts out.

I spent more time than I should have at The Morgue. I ate a pancake and eggs while I changed my shoes and socks. Runners tend to become less modest in this sleep-deprived state of exhaustion. My underwear was the only thing that stayed on as I took off my warm night clothes and exchanged them for shorts and a t-shirt. People think nothing about a gangly guy standing there in his underwear. Plenty of other runners were doing the same thing, modesty be damned.

I saw Mel and Jackson for the last time at mile seventy-five. Mel said, "You are doing awesome! We'll see you soon!" I reminded her that the word "soon" was relative. The prospect of covering another twenty-five miles in my condition seemed virtually impossible.

The thought of a second day in the suffocating heat petrified me. I went into the race well-trained and injury-free, but still found myself close to cutoffs. Unless you've been in that position, it's hard to understand that terrifying fear that you might not make it to the finish in time even though you've worked so hard and pushed your body to the absolute limit. Each aid station has a cutoff time. If you reach that aid station past the cutoff, whether it is an hour or five minutes past, you will be pulled from the race. Even if you've already covered ninety miles. I was up against cutoffs and needed to hustle for the last twenty-five miles if I was going to finish in time.

My companion for the last twenty-five miles was my friend Catherine. When my pervious pacer, Jared, passed the torch to her, I heard him quietly whisper, "He can do this, but he's going to have to hurry. He's pretty close to cutoffs, so keep him moving."

When we started down the trail, Catherine said, "I'll go first. I'm not going to keep a pace that will kill you, but we're going to stay steady. As long as you stay with me, you'll finish before the cutoff."

I couldn't count how many miles we've run together over the years. I'm positive that she's never seen me in such rough shape. I felt sheepish that even the slightest effort had me completely out of breath. I apologized for the involuntary whimpering that would occasionally leave my mouth because my feet, knees, calves, and quads were angry. At that point, the only thing that wasn't hurting on my body was my belly button. It was a tremendous relief and comfort knowing that I didn't have to think about pace and could trust in her to get me to the finish if I worked hard to stay with her.

That last quarter of the race was monumentally difficult. It was relentlessly hot, the trails were unfathomably challenging, and I had already been racing for more than twenty-four hours. At mile eighty-three, I hit a very dark spot. There was absolutely no way I was going to quit, but I could not wrap my head around how I would be able to go another seventeen miles. My body felt demolished. I focused on doing the only thing within my power: continue putting one foot in front of the other. My only purpose was to stay with Catherine, who was bounding effortlessly down the trail like a gazelle who just drank a Red Bull. Meanwhile I felt like sloth that just consumed a bottle of Ambien.

I kept pushing as hard as I could (if you could have seen my "pushing as hard as I could" pace, you would have laughed) and in the final hour of the race I crossed the finish line with a time of thirty-five hours and twenty-five minutes — a mere thirty-five minutes before the cutoff. I was overtaken with gratitude for my crew and pacers, who helped me realize this dream.

So many times during those hundred miles, I asked myself what keeps me coming back to running ultramarathons. In the middle of races like this, it's pretty easy to question your sanity. As I thought about what brought me to the start line of the Wasatch 100, and what kept me going when things got tough, I think it boiled down to one thing: the harder you work for something, the more it means to you. The fact that a hundred miles is monumentally difficult makes the finish line that much sweeter. Being challenged makes you stronger.

The belt buckle you're given at the end of a hundred-miler is a reminder of the time when you pushed yourself to the absolute limit. And then found out that you could push yourself one step farther.

26) "Fast" Cory Is A Fraud

A perspective from the back of the pack

My son Jackson was working on his cycling merit badge. After work on a warm May evening, I joined Jackson and his crew of Scouts on their fifteen-mile ride. It felt a little bit like teaching a group of cats how to ride in a straight line. They were slowly building their mileage, eventually working up to the final merit badge requirement of doing a fifty-mile ride.

I talked with the merit badge counselor before the ride and offered to bring up the rear so that he could lead the group. A crisp line of bikes strung ahead of you is a beautiful thing. And even as the ride began, I could see one boy struggling to keep up.

Terrence was on a small single-speed BMX bike. While everyone else's bike gears were clicking up and down with the terrain, Terrence's bike had no clicking. He pushed the one gear as hard as he could. He pedaled to the point of exhaustion before slowing to a crawl to catch his breath. This scene repeated over and over again. Soon, it was only me and Terrance riding together while the rest of the group sailed effortlessly far ahead. The distance between us and the lead group continued to grow.

When we reached the big hills, Terrance's legs were fried. His slow pedaling soon became slow walking. I rode next to him as he walked. We had lots of time to talk together. The rest of the group was so far ahead that we couldn't see them.

Terrence was far behind. But you know what? It wasn't because he wasn't trying. He was working really hard. In fact, I believe he was actually working harder than the rest of us who had the luxury of things such as gears. The rest of us could sail far with a few easy pedal strokes, while each pedal stroke on Terrence's bike was labored and difficult.

I felt a bond with Terrence as we lingered at the back of the pack because, really, we were kindred souls. I know the back of the pack well. In nearly every race I run, I am well acquainted with the back of the pack. I know that little sting of frustration when I am working hard but I am so far back. I know that little taste of discouragement when, despite your best efforts, everyone is cruising up ahead like they are riding ten-speed bikes while you are stuck on a rusty BMX.

I contend that those of us in the back of the pack really are working as hard as the people in the front. Who knows, maybe harder. Maybe we just have really crappy BMX bikes we're trying to work with. Maybe we're the brave ones — those of us who take the risk to register for a race we're not sure we can finish.

When we finished the ride, Terrance said, "That was fun. Thanks for staying with me." He didn't know how familiar I am with the back of the pack. I actually don't know how to be anywhere else.

* * *

I have not forgotten a post I saw years ago on Facebook after an acquaintance finished a marathon. I found her comment hurtful and offensive. She said, "Well, I finished the St. George Marathon today in a dismal 3:48. I guess that's what happens when you don't train at all and then run with a torn knee meniscus."

I think I felt so sensitive about her comment because I thought to myself, "I *did* train. I trained really hard for many months before that very same marathon. And I ran that exact same race without a torn meniscus. And yet, despite all my preparation and training, I was nowhere near a 3:48 marathon.

Her comment reminded me that the words "fast" and "slow" are relative. A finishing time that was disappointing, embarrassing, and "slow" for her would have left me feeling on top of the world. As much as I disliked her comment, I find myself doing the same thing in my head. I look at race standings and see that I'm generally toward the back. I start to feel inadequate as a runner because I feel like so many people are much better runners than me. A quick glance at my Ultrasignup.com page will show that "Fast Cory" is more of a tongue-in-cheek saying.

The root of this disservice to ourselves and others is comparison. We (okay, I) look at other runners and feel inadequate because they are faster or more athletic or can run longer. But if we insist on playing the comparison game, it might serve us better to compare ourselves to the nation as a whole. Then we might more easily acknowledge the amazing things we are doing.

As runners, we tend to gravitate toward things such as pace and finish times because they are easily quantifiable. We like to have results that are easily measurable because it helps us see how we compare to others. We want to be fast. But pace and finishing time don't measure things like work ethic, dedication, and determination. Even though those characteristics can't be measured, they are every bit as admirable as fast finish times.

Fortunately, the level of fun we are able to have isn't determined by finishing time. Often we go into a race with a goal of a certain finish time in mind. For many races, instead of having a certain finish time goal, my goal for the race is to have an absurd, ridiculous, obscene amount of fun. For example, don't even wear a watch. Legitimately disregard how fast you are going. The only pace you need to focus on is going conservatively enough to have a ridiculous amount of fun.

This is much easier said than done. It's one thing to say "I just want to finish" when someone asks about your goal time. But it's a completely different matter to abandon the concept of time altogether and strive only to enjoy the experience.

I firmly believe that a goal doesn't have to be based on a certain finish time to be a worthy goal. The races where my only purpose is to have an obscene amount of fun are the ones that create the most positive memories. In five years, you won't care one bit about what your finishing time was. (And certainly nobody else cares about your finishing time.) What will stick with you five years later are the times you stopped to enjoy the scenery. That time you paused on the edge of a mesa at sunset to take a picture. That time you were holding your aching stomach because you were laughing so hard with your friend in the middle of a race.

So don't worry about how fast or slow you are. Running is about so much more than speed. More than anything else, I focus on making my running and my racing fun, even if my finishing place is nowhere near first.

27) It Started With The Conversation We Had During Seinfeld

Quadruple St. George Marathon, 2015

W e were lying in bed watching a Seinfeld episode. It was the episode about the marine biologist, and we were howling with laughter. Because all important marital decisions should be discussed over Seinfeld episodes, I paused the show and turned to Mel. "Registration for the St. George Marathon is coming up. I'm thinking about registering, but then running a quadruple marathon. I could start the day before the race, and hopefully be at the starting line to do the last marathon with the actual race." The right corner of her mouth inched upward. "You are crazy. You should do it!"

For a year, one of my goals was to be the first person to run a quadruple St. George Marathon. The plan: start running at the finish line, run up to the start, then back down the course, then once again to the start, hopefully arriving in time to run the last marathon with the official race. The total would be 104.8 miles. It seemed like a unique challenge.

I hate asking for help from others. My original plan was to plant food and water along the course so I wouldn't have to be a burden on Mel. When I told her my intention, she said, "No way! I can schedule to take the day off work and then I can crew for you." I tried to protest, but she insisted. She planned to crew for the first two marathons. The third marathon would be in the middle of the night, when I would run from the finish line up to the starting line again. I told her that I would put a few stashes of food and water along the course to get me through the night.

In the days leading up to the run, I made my final preparations. I bought snacks to keep in the car and a few to hide along the course: Snickers, Oreos, crackers, granola bars, and Mountain Dew. All are easily ingestible, calorie-dense snacks. It's a fairly certain bet that if a food is "calorie dense," I'm in love with it. I also bought gallon bottles of water that Mel could use to mix Tailwind drinks — another favorite fuel.

In the final day before the run, I arranged a few changes of clothes. I drove the course and hid food and water that I could use for marathon number three when I was alone. I hid a change of clothes and a small blanket at the starting line area because I had no idea how accurate my timing would be once I arrived for my fourth marathon. I didn't know whether I'd end up waiting at the starting line for hours, or if I'd even make it to the starting line on time.

The St. George Marathon is always the first Saturday in October. I started my journey early on Friday in the morning darkness. St. George Running Center owner Steve Hooper surprised me and showed up to run the first few miles with me and wish me well.

After a few miles, darkness slowly faded and my surroundings lit up. The sunrise made the red mountains of Snow Canyon State Park glow on the horizon. As I ran through an expanse of red and white sandstone mountains, I couldn't help but be overwhelmed by the beauty of the area where I live.

The St. George Marathon is notorious for being a fast downhill course. But when you're going the opposite direction, a fast downhill course becomes a slow uphill course. For safety, I ran on a bike path next to the highway. While the bike path has the added advantage of being away from traffic, it has an enormous disadvantage of adding more mileage and more climbing. The bike path winds back and forth, and follows the ever changing ups and downs of the terrain it is built upon. Taking the bike path made my total mileage closer to one hundred and eight miles.

My plan for the first couple marathons was to keep a very conservative pace, manage the heat, and have fun. The part of this whole adventure that scared me the most was making the cutoff on the last marathon. If runners are not at mile twenty-three within six hours fifteen minutes, they are pulled from the course. No ifs, ands, or blisters. Some may argue that a 16:13-minute-per-mile pace sounds downright pedestrian. But with seventy-eight miles on your legs, 16:13-per-mile is closer to a speed workout. I knew I needed to pace myself for the first three marathons to make sure I had enough gas in the tank to get me through the last marathon.

During this stage of life, Mel was in graduate school to earn a nurse practitioner Master's degree. She brought her computer and lots of books to keep her busy while she was crewing. She would meet me, refill my hydration pack, make sure I had what I needed, and then drive five or six miles up the road to wait for me while she studied and did homework. It was a comfort knowing that I wasn't out there alone.

As seems to be a theme in a majority of the ultramarathons I've run, it was roasting hot all day. Though I was consuming mostly liquid calories, Mel met me at the official race starting line, which was the finish of my first marathon. She had a bag of Hostess Donettes — the kind that are covered with thick powdered sugar. I don't know what came over me. I started acting like a prisoner of war who hadn't eaten in five days. I couldn't stuff those things in my mouth fast enough.

Running up and down the course the day before the official race, I saw a side of the marathon I had never seen before. I was able to watch a countless army of people preparing for more than seven-thousand people to pass through the next day. Portable toilets were being set up, the road was being cleared of rocks and garbage, and a grandstand of seats was assembled at the finish line for spectators. I also saw the excitement of people who drove up the course to hang signs for their friends or family members who would be running.

While running marathon number two, I passed through the small farming town of Veyo. In the state of Utah, it is illegal to pass through Veyo without stopping for pie at the famous Veyo Pies. I had no interest in breaking the law, so I obliged and made a quick mid-run pit stop at Veyo Pies. The piece of sour cream lemon pie tasted like it had been made by the hands of angels. It's difficult to say whether or not this was a wise decision. Although it was delicious at the time, for the next few miles it felt as though I had ingested a bowling ball.

After twelve hours of running, I was getting tired. My legs had become grumpy. I passed the velvet ropes and punched my one-way ticket into the pain cave. The usual voices of doubt began piping up inside my mind. "If I'm feeling like this now, how in the world am I going to keep going for another ten or twenty more hours?" Those voices can be debilitating and paralyzing. I turned up my music and tried to tune them out.

One. Foot. In. Front. Of. The. Other.

It was dark by the time I finished my second marathon. Mel had stopped to buy a sandwich for me. While I was standing on the sidewalk in the darkness eating the sandwich, a car pulled up. Our friends Amber Farmer, Nicole Stout, and Amanda Jocelyn hopped out. "We've been trying to track you down, Cory! You've already finished two marathons?" They were running the official marathon in the morning and stopped to lend some encouragement, and bring a special treat: a pack of Twinkies.

After I changed clothes, Mel headed home for the night and I began my third marathon. I headed back up the course in hopes of reaching the start line in time to begin the final marathon with the official race. There were a few times during the night that I severely struggled to stay awake. I desperately wanted to lay down and sleep. But I perked up when I started seeing signs that Mel had secretly posted along the course. My eyes may have started to leak a little bit when I saw a sign that said, "Fast Cory Is My Hero."

I smiled to think that in a few short hours, thousands of people would be running down this road. But for now, it was only me, alone by the light of my headlamp. As I listened to my music, it was as though I completely forgot that I was in the middle of a hundred-miler when certain songs took me back in time. A Billy Joel song came on, and I immediately found myself sitting at Billy Joel's concert, which Jackson and I had attended the year before. When a Coldplay song began playing, I was suddenly standing in the kitchen with Danica during one of our random but frequent dance parties. When I heard the country song "Watching Airplanes" by Gary Allen, I was tucking Kylee into bed with a hug and kiss and some tickles. She loved that song so much when she was a little girl and always wanted to listen to it before bed. I was thankful for those happy memories during a difficult part of the hundred-mile run.

Around mile seventy, I had to stop and patch up my feet. At the Wasatch 100 three weeks prior, I made a dumb mistake by not dumping some sand out of my shoes in the middle of a race. Consequently, I finished that race not only receiving a belt buckle, but also taking home some hefty blisters for race souvenirs. By mile seventy of the Quadruple St. George Marathon, those old Wasatch blisters were born again. And then those blisters gave birth to more blisters on top of the old blisters.

So I guess you could say I'm a blister grandfather. How special. Feel free to call me "Grandpa."

I knew it was getting closer to race time when I started seeing busses drive past me. The shoulder on the side of the road is very narrow. It didn't seem at all safe to run on the shoulder of the road with cars and busses passing by. To stay safe, I ran far off the side of the road. But this meant running on a steep slant through tall weeds and thorns. The final ten miles to the start line were like this, and it was miserable. My shoes were full of weeds and thorns, and my ankles and knees took a beating because of the slant.

After what felt like an eternity, I finished the third marathon. I made it to the starting line about an hour and a half before the official start. This gave me time to change my socks, eat the Snickers bars and Mountain Dew I had stashed the day before, and talk with friends.

I knew the final marathon would be the hardest because there was a cutoff I had to make to avoid being pulled from the race. I already had more than eighty miles on my legs, and they weren't working the way they did twenty-four hours earlier. I would have to push as hard as I could to meet the cutoff. To avoid wasting time stopping at aid stations, I wore my UltrAspire hydration pack filled with seventy ounces of fluid so I would only occasionally need to stop for refills.

In the first few miles of the final marathon, I was overcome with anxiousness. My blister grandchildren were giving me fits. My legs were sore and felt like they had turned into old, worn-out wooden boards. I was so scared that I would travel one hundred and two miles to the only race cutoff time, and then be disqualified three miles before the finish line.

In my head I had a conversation with myself. I made a conscious choice that I would need to tune out the soreness and exhaustion, and push forward the best I could. I prayed over and over again for strength and courage. I was once again sitting in my all-too-familiar spot inside the pain cave. I got to the downhill part of the course and was determined that I would do whatever I needed to do to make the cutoff.

When I was at mile ninety-seven (mile eighteen of the official marathon), I heard a voice say, "Hey Cory!" I turned around and saw my friend Rick Whitelaw, followed by Turd'l Miller from the Ultra Adventures race organization. I'd run many, many miles with these guys in the past and had come to truly love them. They also happened to be doing a double St. George marathon to raise money for Girls On The Run.

They said they wanted to run to the finish with me. "No, I don't think you should. I don't want to hold you guys back," I said.

But they insisted. Turd'l said, "We're tired too and we aren't going to be going any faster than we're going now." I didn't know if he was lying or not, but I was overwhelmed with their generosity and support. When your legs have carried you ninety-seven miles, you've been in the heat for two days, and you're sleep deprived, emotions run raw. I told them I was so thankful for their kindness that I might start crying. They said they didn't care.

We came across one more sign as we neared the cutoff. It said, "100.6 miles down. 4.2 to go!" I smiled thinking about my sweet wife and family. (Incidentally, after the race, I heard quite a few runners tell me they saw that sign and thought, "What in the world is that sign talking about?") Tears streamed from my eyes when I realized that we were going to make the cutoff. I was overcome with gratitude and joy.

Mel and Kylee had volunteered at an aid station throughout the day but left early enough to be at the finish line as I crossed. The announcer on the loud speaker happened to be a friend who knew about my shenanigans. When I finished, he announced that I had just completed the first-ever quadruple St. George Marathon. While this was a very kind gesture, it almost got me in trouble.

Another runner heard that I had just finished a hundred-plus mile run. She came over to congratulate me, and then went into a long lesson about everything she had learned by reading the book "Born To Run." I appreciated that she was interested in ultrarunning, but right after finishing those hundred and eight miles, my body shut down and I felt like I was on the verge of a vomit volcano. She kept talking, but I didn't want to be rude and tell her I needed to go sit down. While she expounded on the incredible running feats of the Tarahumara Indians, the only thing that kept repeating in my mind was, "Please don't throw up on her shoes. Please don't throw up on her shoes. Please don't throw up on her shoes."

When she finished talking, I stumbled over to a patch of grass and collapsed in a dehydrated mess. "You don't look very good right now," Mel said. Kylee ran and grabbed a garbage can to set next to me just in case I did toss my cookies. I laid there on the grass for a long time looking up at the sky while trying to coax my stomach to regain its composure.

Any ultrarunner knows that making it to the finish line of a race vomit-free is as much a cause for celebration as is running the distance. On the drive home we celebrated with a stop for ice cream.

28) So Many Selfie Sticks

Grand Canyon Rim to Rim to Rim, 2015

One of the items on the bucket list of many trail runners is to run rim to rim to rim — or "R2R2R" in the Grand Canyon. Essentially, runners start at one rim of the Grand Canyon, run down, into, and across the canyon floor, then up to the other rim before turning around to go back. In November 2015, I was able to put a check mark next to that goal.

The year before, I ran the Grand Canyon 100 mile race. The course led us along the edge of the Grand Canyon with views that left my running partners Catherine, Clair, Jared, and I speechless. But that race never went inside the actual canyon.

Most R2R2R runners and hikers start at the South Rim of the Grand Canyon. This is due to a few factors including the fact that the South Rim is accessible all year, while the North Rim is closed during the winter because of its higher elevation and snow. There are also many more lodging options at the South Rim. The North Rim has sweeping, panoramic views of the canyon, but the South Rim has the views that the Grand Canyon is known for, with a dozen viewpoints to the Colorado River down below. The South Rim sees around four million visitors each year compared to less than one million at the North Rim.

I opted to start at the North Rim because of its proximity. I can drive to the North Rim from my house in two and a half hours, versus more than four hours to the South Rim. I made the trip alone and didn't have any crew support or provisions meeting me at the South Rim, so I packed everything I thought I might possibly need for the entire journey. My hydration pack was stuffed to the brim with a jacket, gloves, candy bars, a small first aid kit, sunscreen, and an extra bottle of water.

On the drive to the Grand Canyon, I considered the possibility that I may have to cancel my run. It was pouring rain all day, and when I arrived at the North Rim, snow was falling from the sky and the trees were covered in a blanket of white.

At four in the morning, the alarm on my watch started beeping. It was freezing in the back of my Dodge Durango where I had been sleeping, and it took tremendous willpower to remove my body from the warm sleeping bag. I ate a bowl of Raisin Bran, a banana, a granola bar, and a bottle of orange juice. Then I strapped on my pack, laced up my shoes, and hit the trail to start my Grand Canyon adventure.

The trailhead was pitch black and there was not another solitary soul anywhere in the area. I clicked on my headlamp, walked up the parking lot, and then started on the trail that was near some bathrooms. Having never run here before, this was the only trail I saw. I ran in peaceful silence for a time, then thought, "Hmm, I've been running for quite a while. It seems like I should have started dropping into the canyon by now."

I passed a trail junction sign. It said the Ken Patrick Trail was one way, and the Uncle Jim Trail was the other way. "Okay. That is really strange. Neither of those options are the North Kaibab Trail which I am supposed to be on."

Was there another trail I could have taken? I hadn't seen any. So I just kept running. After another ten minutes I stopped. I thought, "I really don't think this is the right way. But I don't want to turn around and run all the way back to the parking lot if this actually is the right way to go. Then I would have to cover all this mileage again! But I definitely don't want to keep going on this trail if it's the wrong way."

I weighed all my options, then turned around and ran back to the parking lot. As I returned, a car was pulling into the parking lot. I walked up and asked the two guys in the car if they knew where the North Kaibab Trail was. They said they were hiking to the South Rim, but had never been here before so they didn't know either. We explored everywhere around the upper parking lot, but kept ending up in mule corrals or near cabins that had been abandoned for the winter.

By this time I was extremely frustrated. I had lost valuable time searching for the trail, and had added many miles to my legs before even starting. We finally went down the parking lot instead of going up, and saw the sign for the North Kaibab Trail.

The total length of the trail from the North Rim to the South Rim (via the Bright Angel Trail) is forty-six miles (That is, of course, if you're not a moron who gets lost before the run even starts). The descent into the mouth of the Grand Canyon was rocky and steep. With every passing mile I thought to myself, "Wow, this is going to hurt when I come back up this trail!"

Before running here, I didn't know that over the course of those forty-six miles, the trail crosses many rivers and streams with bridges built above them that hikers can cross. I was close to the bottom of the canyon when the first light of day started touching the top of the cliffs. The scenery was so incredible that I couldn't help but stop to take pictures. I quickly realized that none of the pictures I was taking seemed to truly capture the beauty of the moment. I gave up and put the camera back in my pocket. The Grand Canyon is too expansive to capture in a single picture.

Thanks to the amazing Grand Canyon R2R2R Facebook group, I knew that it was important to take a little sidetrack route to see Ribbon Falls. I heard that the views were certainly worth the extra mileage. After coming around a corner and seeing Ribbon Falls for myself, I wholeheartedly agreed. Crystal clear water poured from a towering peak high above me. Streams of whitewater hit the rocks below, which were covered in brilliant green moss. I hadn't seen another person on the trail that day, so I had time to enjoy the falls all to myself.

While running rim to rim to rim, I was surprised by two things:

1) The trail going up and down the canyon is really, really steep;
2) The trail at the bottom of the canyon is very runnable. The entire trail that runs along the bottom of the canyon is nearly smooth, and there is minimal elevation gain. It is virtually flat compared to the trails that lead in and out of the canyon.

There are periodic water faucets throughout the length of the canyon to accommodate hikers and mule riders. There were some repairs on the water pipeline during the day of my run, and some water faucets were turned off for the year. Since I didn't know how often I would have access to water I tried to conserve, and didn't drink nearly as much as I should have. I later paid dearly for this.

At the bottom of the canyon is a little compound called Phantom Ranch. They have some small bunk cabins, a campground, and tiny store where you can pay fourteen dollars for a sack lunch. I'd heard that it is mandatory to buy lemonade from Phantom Ranch. If not, they take your firstborn child, give you paper cuts between your toes, and make you listen to Celine Dion music. I didn't want any of those things to happen, so I bought some lemonade.

As I was running, I heard an airplane fly high above me. I thought about how amazing the Grand Canyon must look from thirty-thousand feet. And then I thought about how incredibly lucky I was at that very moment to be standing right in the middle of that amazingness.

By this point I was right in the heart of the canyon. I was feeling fairly good overall. For years I've gazed in envy at pictures of runners at the enormous suspension bridge that crosses the Colorado River. It was so cool to finally be there myself.

Soon enough I began the ascent up to the South Rim via the South Kaibab Trail. I am deathly scared of heights. So at certain points I had to really stay focused on the trail two feet in front of me — ignoring the fact that this trail was right on the edge of a cliff — while repetitively whispering, "Don't. Die. Don't. Die. Don't. Die."

As I got closer to the South Rim, I started seeing campers. And hiking tourists. And large quantities of selfie sticks. So. Many. Selfie. Sticks. And a mule train. Ah, the smell of mule urine in the afternoon.

With the whole "Oh crap, I'm lost" incident at the beginning of the day and the detour to Ribbon Falls, I was farther behind schedule than I preferred. Then dehydration caught up with me. I felt completely worn out. When I finally reached the South Rim, I was apprehensive about turning around and going back into the canyon. I can't put into words how daunting it is to drop into the bottom of the Grand Canyon, climb your way out, and then stare at the wide open mouth of the canyon you are about to drop back into again.

I did some self-talk and reminded myself that I was in the midst of something I had wanted to do for a long time. I was doing something I would be proud of myself for. I am strong. I am brave. I can do this. I CAN DO THIS. Plus, there was that minor detail that I didn't have another way to travel back to the North Rim, aside from calling Mel and saying, "Hey, want to come and pick me up at the South Rim?" But by the time she drove more than four hours to come get me, then four hours back, I could run back to my car. So I turned around and entered the Grand Canyon, again.

Somewhere in the bottom of the canyon, something terrible happened. I had been running with my nice hundred-dollar Black Diamond trekking poles. And then I realized that I wasn't running with my trekking poles. CRAP! I must have set them down when I went to the bathroom and forgot to retrieve them. I figured they were about a mile and a half back. "Should I turn around and get them, or just leave them?" I wondered. I didn't want any more extra mileage, and I certainly didn't want to add extra time in the canyon since night was approaching. But I couldn't leave those expensive poles, so I turned around to get them.

Unfortunately they weren't where I thought I left them. CRAP! So I added *another* three extra miles, and still lost my poles. The forty-six mile R2R2R run was now closer to fifty-three miles. That foolish mistake ate at me every step of the rest of the run.

I passed by Phantom Ranch again on the return trip. Watching the sun set on the canyon was breathtakingly beautiful. I had many more hours alone in the dark as I climbed out of the canyon and up to the North Rim. It was cold and windy. I was having a hard time staying awake. I struggled so much to keep my eyes open that I thought, "I'm just going to lay here on the trail for twenty minutes and take a quick power nap. I clicked off my headlamp, but the pitch dark was too suffocating, and I feared I was making myself too appealing as a late night snack for a mountain lion. So I turned the headlamp back on and closed my eyes for a quick nap. Within thirty seconds, I knew sleep wasn't going to happen because my body was quivering and shaking from the cold.

Between the extra miles and hundreds of photo opportunities, I ended up taking between seventeen to eighteen hours to complete the journey. I crawled into the makeshift bed in the back of my Durango and slept like a baby. I woke up a few hours later at the light of day and looked back into the Grand Canyon, full of gratitude for such an amazing experience.

29) I Was The Guy In The Cat Leotard

Across The Years, 2016

My dad died when he was thirty-eight years old. Ever since I started running ultramarathons, I wanted to run one at age thirty-eight to honor him. At the end of 2015, I returned to Across The Years to do just that. I had turned thirty-eight a few weeks before the race. As a kid, my dad seemed so, well, old. He listened to the kind of music that old people listened to. He drove the kind of car that old people drive. His once black hair was being overrun by gray. On the day I turned thirty-eight myself, I had a realization that now I am the one who listens to old-people music. I drive an old-people car. My once jet black hair is becoming less jet black by the day. But on my birthday, I didn't feel old. I felt young and alive. I realized that this is why I run. Those hours on the trails, those miles of fresh air make me feel alive. I wished more than anything that my dad could feel what I was feeling at age thirty-eight, instead of being trapped inside a broken body. I would run Across The Years for him.

Mel was bombarded with school and work, so Jackson came along again for another crewing adventure. During the six-hour drive to Phoenix, we laughed a lot, ate the kind of fast food that probably shouldn't be consumed before a three-day ultramarathon, and listened to Bruce Springsteen music loud enough to make our ears ring.

After arriving in Phoenix, we headed to the race course at Camelback Ranch. We set up our camp next to the track in what would be our home for the coming seventy-two hours. I hoped to not spend too much time on the inside of that tent. When we arrived, the six-day race had already started. I was happy to see friends from the previous year, and couldn't help but feel excited while wondering how I would do when my race started the next day.

The next morning, I stood with a group of runners at the starting line, waiting for the race to begin. My goal going into the race was to beat the two-hundred and five miles I had run the year before. I knew everything would need to go almost perfectly for seventy-two hours in order for that to happen, but it was what I wanted to shoot for.

At the starting line of most races, you'll find friendly conversations, banter, and laughing. Usually, once the race starts, conversations end and people get down to business. But the atmosphere at Across The Years is different. With a course that consists of a 1.05-mile loop run over and over again, those friendly conversations and banter don't stop once the race starts. We were able to have interactions with the same people throughout the race.

A few months before Across The Years, I found a hideously absurd cat unitard — a skin-tight piece of clothing similar to a wrestling singlet with the face of a fluffy kitten on front and back. I figured I'd bring it to the race to wear for a few miles and hopefully distract runners from their grumpy legs.

At about four in the afternoon on day one, I made a quick stop at the tent to change into the cat suit. Once dressed, I stood there in the tent thinking. "Can I really bring myself to walk out of the tent looking like this to run a few laps?" It seemed like a decision I would regret. It seemed like a decision I would look back on as a poor life choice. And I was convinced I would immediately be forced to surrender my Man Card once I stepped outside the tent. I finally mustered the courage to slowly unzip the tent and resume running on the course.

Some people seemed shocked to see my scrawny, white body covered in a skin-tight cat unitard. But most people laughed and said they loved it. I was surprised how many people came up and said something like, "I've been going through a rough stretch but seeing your cat suit made me smile. I needed something to make me smile right now. Thanks!" Even if they were thinking it, nobody formally asked me to surrender my Man Card. I believe I may have found the only thing that could make runners' eyes hurt worse than their legs. The cat suit made it three miles before I returned to the tent to change back into my running clothes.

With a timed race like this, you can rest or sleep whenever you want. Similar to the previous year, my plan was to go through the first night without sleeping. The first nigh was bitter, bitter cold. One runner said his car showed that it was twenty-seven degrees. Do you want to know something that is not the slightest bit awesome? Twenty-seven degrees. Since when did Phoenix, Arizona, become hospitable to polar bears? I was incredibly thankful when the sun finally started to rise on day two.

I finished the first twenty-four hours with a total of eighty miles. After those first twenty-four hours, I felt like a patient from the middle ages who was given leeches to drain their blood. But instead of feeling like leeches had sucked my blood, it felt as though they had sucked out my energy. I was completely drained. I wasn't overly concerned about this because it's normal to go through highs and lows, but I hoped my energy would return soon.

One of the greatest distractions to combat the toll of compounding miles was to visit with other runners who were going through their own highs and lows. I enjoyed talking with my friend Patrick Sweeney, who had run across the country the year before. I enjoyed talking with eighty-one-year-old Barbara Macklow, who completed a remarkable seventy-nine miles in the two-day race. I enjoyed spending many miles talking with David Johnston, who won the previous year's six-day race by running 551 miles! (No, that is not a typo.) Now he was running the six-day race again. David is a witty, unassuming runner from Alaska. The miles I spent with him were like running with a superstar, though he would never see himself this way. He's one of the most humble, unpretentious people I've met.

As we ran, David told me stories of his adventures running in his home state of Alaska. "We always carry bear spray when we run up there. You probably won't need it, but you definitely don't want to be without it if you get into a bad situation. One time I was on a training run with my friend. He was behind me a little bit when all of the sudden I heard a blood-curdling scream. My mind was racing with everything that could have happened as I ran back to him, but I knew it was bad. When I got to him, I saw that he had tripped and punctured his can of bear spray, and it had sprayed him right in the crotch!" Both of us were howling with laughter as he told the story. "Yeah, he stripped his clothes off as fast as he could and then ran over and jumped in the ice cold river to wash off. I'm telling you, man, every run in Alaska is a crazy adventure."

I used mostly liquid calories during the run, but I also didn't shy away from food at the aid station when I felt hungry. The Across The Years aid station is the best I've ever seen. They had staple foods available twenty-four hours a day, but even more food at meal times. I loved having a hot bowl of oatmeal each morning. I ate pizza, sub sandwiches, cookies, and tamales that were so spicy that I was scared they would burn a hole through my intestines.

By the afternoon of the second day, I was in one of those low points where loneliness, despair, frustration, and discouragement try to suffocate you. I was sleepy, worn out, and every cell of my body was throwing an uproarious temper tantrum. (I realize this may sound exaggerated, but I assure you that being in the midst of running for three days will leave you feeling this way.) For the first time at any of my races, I brought a picture of my dad that I had tucked away in a drop bag. I pulled out that picture during this difficult time to remind me why I was running.

The typical foot neuropathy I feel during hundred-plus-mile runs was raging with a fury. Every step felt like a combination of walking on needles and red-hot coals. I've yet to find anything that makes it better once it kicks in.

It was surely a good omen when the sound system at the main aid station turned the music on the satellite radio to the Bruce Springsteen station. They turned the music up loud and left it there for hours. Every time I came through the aid station and heard a new Bruce Springsteen song, I was reminded of my drive to Phoenix with Jackson.

A few hours later, I broke out the cat suit for two more miles. I don't always wear a hideously absurd cat suit during an ultramarathon, but when I do, I take a jumping picture. I assumed that the cat suit would likely never again see the light of day, so I figured I better take the opportunity to get a jump shot with a singlet so tight that it looked like I had a kitten painted on my body.

Jackson was a helpful crew leader. He kept my bottles refilled so that when I stopped by my personal aid station, I always had a drink ready to go. He walked over to the store across the street and returned with a candy bar to surprise me. He also came out on the course to do a few miles with me every once in a while. By this point I wasn't going very fast. As we walked, he told me stories of runners he had seen coming through the aid station, or scores from that day's basketball games. Over the three days, he ended up getting in a total of fourteen miles.

During the late nineteenth century, six-day races were hugely popular sporting events. Back then, the elite six-day racers were like the Michael Jordan and LeBron James of our day. I still regard them this way. What's so impressive is that the Michael Jordan and LeBron James of ultrarunning are the nicest, most down-to-Earth guys you could ever meet. I feel so fortunate to be able to call these guys friends.

Case in point: Ed "The Jester" Ettinghausen who is one of my running heroes. Not only is he supportive, friendly, and kind, but he is also an amazing runner. Ed told me stories about running Badwater — a 135-mile ultramarathon held in Death Valley during the heat of summer — and gave me tips for the race if I ever decided to run it. He said, "I've only offered to do this with two other people, but if you want to run it, I'd be happy to write a letter of recommendation for you. I think you'd be perfect for that race."

I was humbled by his gesture, and told him that I may just take him up on his offer in a few months when the application period opened for Badwater. (Ed ended up winning this year's six-day race by running a remarkable 481 miles.

I was incredibly sleepy after not sleeping at all the first night, so I went to our tent in hopes of catching a few hours of sleep. Unfortunately, the second night was just as cold as the first night. I laid in my sleeping bag covered by a pile of blankets but still felt frozen to the core. I was so cold that I'd fall asleep for a bit but then wake myself up again shivering. It was approximately as enjoyable as getting a root canal from a dentist who is covered in cat hair. Eventually I decided to just get up and start walking again. The problem was that I was so tired and sore that I couldn't move fast enough to generate much heat. If I was in the tent, I was miserably cold. If I was out on the course walking, I was miserably cold. That night was brutal.

After a night that felt like it lasted an entire month, the sun finally rose on day three. Soon afterward, a new batch of twenty-four-hour runners started their race. It was nice to get some fresh blood out on the course and see some runners who weren't (yet) doing the ultra death shuffle.

The latter miles of an ultramarathon are always so inspiring to me. Runners have been in forward motion hour after hour after hour. They are tired, worn down and raw. So, so raw. They are determined, brave, and dedicated. It is really remarkable to see runners who are clearly struggling, but continue to push forward.

In a perfect world where there is a Butterfinger under your pillow every morning, Celine Dion is banned from grocery store sound systems, and unicorns are for sale on Amazon, I would have loved to beat 205 miles. But one of the things I love about ultramarathons is the adventure of never knowing what is going to happen. Results aren't guaranteed. A race can go well or badly, but you'll never know how things will turn out until you muster the gumption to try. I love the uncertainty. I resolved that even if I didn't hit 205 miles, I would keep fighting. My goal was to reach the seventy-two hour cutoff knowing I had given my absolute hundred percent.

By this time, my body felt like I had been fighting in a cage match. Unfortunately I have as much muscle composition as a praying mantis, so my body didn't stand much of a chance in the cage match against Across The Years. In a race that lasts seventy-two hours, you don't need to worry if something is hurting. Just give it a little time and something else will start hurting to take your mind off the first ailment. This little game continues hour after hour, day after day.

On the last night, I fell into a slump where I was sleepwalking at the speed of an elephant stuck in mud. As with the previous nights, it was freezing cold. Dave Johnston, the Alaskan runner who regularly runs though blizzards, zoomed past me and said, "I want to go home. It's too cold here!"

Jackson came out and did some miles with me to get me moving again. I tried to talk him out of it. "Jackson, it is bitter cold out here. It's not going to be fun. I don't mind if you go back to the car and get to bed for the night," I said. But he insisted that it was fun, and he wanted to come out on the course.

By this point I was nearly too tired to formulate sentences, but I managed to mutter, "Okay, what I want you to do is walk ahead of me and I'll do my best to keep up with your pace." I marveled at how effortlessly he was able to walk down the path. I had forgotten what it felt like to move effortlessly. For me, every step was labored and difficult.

I learned my lesson from trying to sleep in the tent for a few hours the night before. I had no interest in laying in a sleeping bag quivering from the cold. On the third night, I did what many other runners were doing: I went to my car, cranked up the heat until it was warm enough to bake bread, and then dozed off to sleep for two hours. In these races, my mind never truly shuts down. It seems to remember that even though I'm tired beyond measure, I'm still in the middle of a race. After a few hours of restlessly shifting around my uncomfortable reclined car seat, I went back to the course.

During the nights at these races, the course becomes far less populated with runners. There are only a handful of runners who aren't in their tents trying to get warm or get some sleep. Those runners on the course push on, mile after mile, into the darkness. When you see a runner far ahead, you know who it is because you've seen each other for so many miles that you have memorized what everyone's running and walking gait looks like. At night, people look less like runners and more like zombies.

Though I wasn't moving very fast, I felt proud of myself for being out on the course during the nights. Those were incredibly difficult parts of the race, and I was happy that I didn't give up. My soul was filled with happiness when I saw the first light of day on the last morning of the race.

I finished Across The Years with a total of one hundred and fifty miles, a number that seemed unreachable during the points of the race when I struggled the most. I'm consistently amazed at what can be accomplished at ultramarathons when you keep moving forward and don't give up. I had just enough energy saved for a jump at the finish line. Across The Years was an inspiring, challenging, rewarding adventure. I tried to imagine what my dad's reaction would have been if he had been there watching the race. I think he would have been proud of me.

30) Conclusion

The equal and opposite reaction of ultrarunning

Running an ultramarathon gives you a crash course in gratitude, patience, perseverance, and the rewarding feeling of knowing you've pushed through walls and come out victorious on the other side. I'm not a particularly gifted athlete, but I am tenacious and stubborn. And in ultrarunning, that can take you a long way.

It is difficult to find a better description of ultramarathons than Isaac Newton's Third Law of Motion: "For every action, there is an equal and opposite reaction." These races take us to the deepest, darkest recesses of pain, loneliness, and despair. But as dark as those moments can become, there is an equal and opposite reaction of pride, satisfaction, and overwhelming happiness that comes after a race.

Do you know what I have loved about the finish lines of ultramarathons that I have run? Often, there is hardly anybody there. There aren't thousands of cheering spectators. There isn't a marching band. No big fireworks show.

There is a small group of people walking around like Frankenstein with huge smiles on their faces. And when you finish, people give you a high five and say "good job." That's it. And it seems so appropriate and fitting because the reward for doing something like this is completely intrinsic. The satisfaction of knowing you pushed yourself way, way, way farther than you once thought possible is more valuable than any cheers from a crowd.

Sometimes when I'm out alone on a trail, I can feel my dad with me. I'd like to think that he has joined me on some of those trails since he passed away. I imagine him breathing in the fresh air, feeling his legs move beneath him, and absorbing the surrounding scenery. I can't help but wonder if that's what continually draws me to ultrarunning. I yearn for those moments when I am struggling, or when my limits are tested, or when I persevere despite overwhelming challenges. Those are the moments when heaven touches Earth and I can feel him beside me.

Acknowledgements

In high school, I had an English teacher named Mr. Gentry. He had a reputation for being the most challenging teacher in the school. He expected nothing but the best, and challenged me to develop myself as a writer. Since then, others have taken a chance on me and encouraged me to share my stories with others. I'm thankful for Jennifer Durrant who gave me an opportunity to write a column for The Spectrum newspaper for many years. John Medinger and Lisa Henson formerly of UltraRunning Magazine provided an opportunity to write for their publication. I am incredibly thankful for the support from current UltraRunning Magazine editor Karl Hoagland.

Many people deserve thanks for helping to bring this book to life. Steve Hooper from St. George Running Center was the person who relentlessly encouraged me to write a book. Jill Homer provided insight to help get a book project off the ground, and edited the book.

Words can't adequately describe the gratitude and love I feel for my family. I'm thankful for my children Jackson, Danica, and Kylee. I'm thankful for the posters they've made at some of my races. I'm thankful for the encouraging letters they've written for me to stash in my pack to read when I am struggling during a race. I'm thankful for their humor, happiness, and kindness that they show each day.

I feel so blessed to have a wife who has been unquestionably supportive of all my running adventures. She has never questioned or discouraged any of my running aspirations. The best decision I ever made was to marry Mel.

Finally, I'm thankful for God and the opportunities he has placed before me. I'm thankful for the body I have been given. It has allowed me to feel my feet move beneath me, breathe fresh air, and experience the beauty of God's creations.

You know what? Thanks!

Thanks for reading the book. Seriously. Thanks! If you were standing here right now, I'd give you a hug and a homemade cinnamon roll. I hope the universe rewards you with good karma in the form of a pot of gold in your backyard, toenails that never turn black after long runs, and a baby pet unicorn.

If you enjoyed "Nowhere Near First," here are a few things you can do now that you've finished the book:

- Head to Amazon, Kindle, or Audible and pick up my book "Into The Furnace: How a 135 Mile Run Across Death Valley Set My Soul on Fire."
- Head over to www.coryreese.com.
- While there, subscribe to the mailing list for new articles, upcoming events, and epic cinnamon roll recipes.
- Tell a friend you think would enjoy "Nowhere Near First."
- Write a social media post. Facebook, Twitter, and blog posts are awesome ways to let people know you liked the book!
- Leave a review at Amazon, Goodreads, or wherever you bought the book. Those help a ton.

I sincerely appreciate your awesomeness.
Sincerely, Cory